D0911489

Créoles of New Orleans

Gens de Couleur
(PEOPLE OF COLOR)

The photographs and writings are from a CETA *Artists in the City of New Orleans Project* and was developed February 1978 through August 1978. Additional interviews were conducted in February 1984.

The work presents a view of the Seventh Ward, also known as *The Créole Section*, of New Orleans, Louisiana, included in which are historical and contemporary facts and fancies about the city and its story.

PHOTOGRAPHS BY OWEN MURPHY   WRITINGS BY LYLA HAY OWEN

The Seventh Ward Work is dedicated, with affection, to "Chuck," without whom it could never have been done, and to The Arts Council of New Orleans.

First Quarter Publishing Company
New Orleans

I

The Créoles of New Orleans
© 1987 First Edition by First Quarter Publishing Company

All rights reserved . No part of this book may be reproduced or transmitted in any form or by any means, electronic or mechanical, including photocopying, recording or by any information storage and retrieval system, without permission in writing from the Publisher.
First Quarter Publishing Company
P.O. Box 52617
New Orleans, La. 70152

ISBN# 0-9408 35-00-2

The Seventh Ward Créoles of New Orleans

The Créoles of Color who once lived in this area of New Orleans in far greater numbers and as a highly structured group seem unfortunately to face future survival only as a cultural phenomenon of the past. Like most inner-city neighborhoods, the seventh ward is also experiencing an exodus of its young adults to the suburbs and finds itself in a state of uncertainty as to its future development and/or life.

The New Orleans Gens de Couleur are members of a distinctly rare group, small in numbers compared to Italian, Jewish or Mexican communities in the United States, but equally high in family and social traditions. Wherever they have moved, they have tried to take their culture along. Be it in Los Angeles or Chicago, they have lent dignity and beauty to the human condition through their existence.

We, the authors, wish to express our gratitude to the many people who invited us into their homes and businesses, to attend their functions and parties, and partake of the generous hospitality which is so prevalent in the Créole Society, in order that we could photograph and interview them for this work.

PREFACE

What is a Créole?

Créole. A familiar word. Everyone knows it. And we all think we know what it means, until we are asked to define it.

Everyone I asked knew the word (though a couple of them associated it only with cooking) and each and every one of them mentioned "French."

There exists a real need for a definitive study of the Créoles, and *Créoles of New Orleans,* Gens de Couleur, fulfills that need superbly. It provides no pat answer to the question, "What is a Créole?", for there is no answer — there is a multitude of answers. And this book presents them all for the reader, all the facts, all the details, all the explanations in all their diversity, with all their contradictions and conflicting viewpoints — and still manages to convey that sense of mystery that has always surrounded the Créole phenomenon.

Living in an age as we do that has a mania for pigeonholing, compartmentalizing, and defining, it is not only instructive and illuminating, but also refreshing and inspiring, to be allowed to enter, during the course of this fascinating book, that elegant, enigmatic society that flourished in a world of its own, partly drawn from both Black and White, yet belonging to neither.

Their song is a part of America, and we have taken their lives into our stream of life without realizing we were doing it. This book gives us a chance to study, acknowledge and celebrate an American group that dates back in time longer than a lot of our other groups do, a group that established a part of our country, a country that was pretty crude and needed taming, a group of people that have never issued warnings of distrust to their neighbors but always let their neighbors in.

You might ask, what is a Créole song? Read this book and you will find out.

You may know a Créole, you may pass one in the street. Their roots are there in New Orleans, but their lives are lived everywhere. This book by Lyla Hay Owen and Owen Murphy gives you an opportunity to learn about your neighbors, and just perhaps, this book will inspire an interest in you to learn more about yourself and your own roots.

John Underwood
Darwin Hageman
Editors of *AVATAR PRESS,*
New York

Introduction
Dedication to the City

There are passages in the book *Memoirs of a Créole*, by Mme. Helene D'Aquin Allain, that reflect some of what I would like to record as a dedication to the city in which I was born . . .

Chère Nouvelle Orléans, Patrie de ma jeunesse, berceau de quelques-uns de mes ancestres, tombeau d' un grand nombre de ceux que j'ai aimés, Je demande à Dieu de te protéger, de te garder, de te bénir.
Par une Créole. 1868

Et maintenant, adieu, chers souvenirs de la Louisiane. Je dis à tous ceux dont il n'est pas fait mention, Ou tous ceux de qui le nom n'est pas inscrit ici: croyez que je ne vous ai pas oubliés. J'ai dû me borner, restreindre mon cadre, voiler plus d'une image, et ce n'étaient pas les moins vivantes; mais je m'ai rien oublié, et chaque amitié a sa place dans le coeur, aussi créole que français, qui vous dit: Au revoir, dans le ciel! Ne m'oubliez pas.
Forget me not!

Dear New Orleans, home of my youth, cradle of many ancestors, tomb of many I have loved, I ask of God to protect, to preserve and to bless thee! From a Créole.

And now, goodbye dear memories of Louisiana. I told everyone whom I didn't mention here to believe that I didn't forget you, but I had to limit my framework and to conceal more than I imagined, and that you weren't less alive to me. I haven't forgotten anything, and each friendship has a place in my heart, my heart, both Créole and French. . . . As you all said . . . till I *see* you in Heaven.
Forget me not!

1868 . . . 1987
Lyla Lagarde

Dedication

This book is also dedicated, with much love and respect, to Charles Story. He acted as our "Guide and Teacher" while we were working in the 7th ward.

His family history winds through the history of New Orleans as naturally and as certainly as the Mississippi River, Lake Pontchartrain, and all the Bayous and waterways wind through and around our city. His mother's family, the Christophe's, was originally from Haiti and was related to the King of Haiti, Henri Christophe. Henri Christophe ruled Haiti from 1811 until 1820, when he committed suicide. Charles was further related to Alderman Sydney Story whose famous namesake was "Storyville," that celebrated red-light district of old "Basin Street Blues" and "House of the Rising Sun" fame. He also claims connection with William Story, the very first King of "Zulu" (The Zulu Social Aid and Pleasure Club), the celebrated Negro Carnival Organization).

Charles Story was born in New Orleans, reared in New Orleans, made pilgrimages outside of the South to Europe and to Los Angeles, but always returned — just as all of the spiritually bound New Orleanians return, much as "spirits" themselves come to the city. For it is said, "New Orleans is the Playground and Vacation Land of all the fun loving souls who have gone over to the next world."

Supposedly, that is why the city never changes. "The Spirits" like New Orleans just the way she is . . . and so she remains . . . unchanging . . . easygoing . . . lush and exotic . . . a little old fashioned and possessing a lot of Joie de Vivre.

What Is A Créole?

New Orleans history has emerged as part fact, part myth and part legend. It has evolved from songs and from stories told by and about "everyone" who ever came to the city. The black slaves, the churches, the whores, soldiers, landed gentry, the Indians, Germans, Africans, Spaniards, Frenchmen, Acadians, Caribbeans, the Irish, all who came helped create the myth . . . the history of New Orleans.

No definitive history has been written about New Orleans. Records of births and deaths, baptisms, documents of all sorts are scattered throughout the world. The churches of France, Haiti, Spain, Quebec, and England contain as many facts concerning the people and history of New Orleans as can be found in New Orleans herself. It would be an almost impossible task for an historian to gather the multifarious documents.

The "Créole" emerged as part of the history and part of the myth of New Orleans. The Créole existed, flourished, "passed like a vapor on the summer air," danced, and sang in the alleys and kitchens of, waited on, bore children by, and by turns was "the Southern Aristocrat."

The Créole helped stir the past, the present, the future of New Orleans. The Créole still exists.

What is a Créole?

You will get as many different answers from as many different people you ask.

What is a Créole?

Call it what you want it to be . . . a mixture of black and white. Too black to be white. Too white to be black.

. . . Free Jacks

That's deep information.

French and Spanish . . . I don't know.

A true Créole? What the white didn't want and the black man couldn't have . . . a Créole . . . a kitchen nigger . . . a house girl.

French, Italian, and Negro . . . Heinz . . . 57 varieties.

Créoles? Créoles have to be black now. This is 1987!

Hmm! I know my mama believed in Voodoo. . . .

Hoodoo!

If you eat gumbo with shrimp and crab . . . you a Créole!

Mixture of Spanish, French and American . . . some say Spanish and French!

What is a Créole?

"A Negro, Indian, Frenchman, Caucasian, and Spanish."

"A French bastard, yes, a Frenchman sired the child."

"Night fightin' . . . sneakin' around."

"French and black. . . . A form."

"Integration that existed 100 years ago."

"Wasn't all by choice . . . Wasn't all by force."

"Well, it was back in 1803 when free men of color were all first referring to themselves as 'Créoles.'"

"Gens de Couleur" . . .

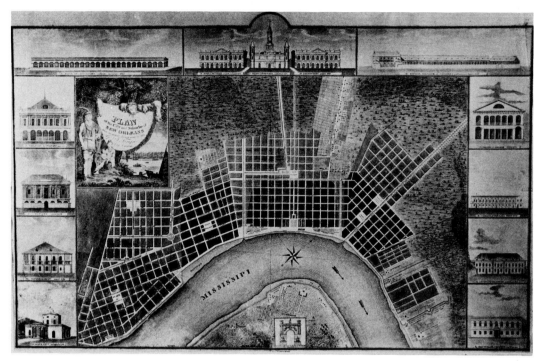

Plan of the City and Suburbs of New Orleans, 1824 by Tanesse
From the Collections of Louisiana State Museum

Créoles of Color

For many years there were laws preventing marriage and/or cohabitation between persons of different races. However, these laws never prevented the begetting of mulatto children by both black and white men with white and black women, nor did it completely prevent the races from cohabitating.

In the South one was never asked whether or not he or she had any "white blood," but rather, if there was any "black blood" in the family history; for one "drop" of black blooded ancestry meant that you were considered "colored," and "colored" was what was indicated as your race on any and all official documents concerning your birth, baptism, marriage, schooling, health, and employment.

For a time, light-complexioned, free people of color were not considered to be the same as blacks. In the early theatres of New Orleans, for example, they had a whole tier, usually the second tier, allotted to them. In 1830 a playhouse opened and operated especially for the "colored population," but the whites were also admitted, and there were special prices for slaves and servants accompanying their masters.

And, of course, there were the quadroons of the opulent and infamous Quadroon Balls, described by the Duke of Saxe-Weimar in the early 1800's.

> "A quadroon is the child of a mestizo mother and a white father,
> as a mestizo is the child of a mulatto mother and a white father.

2

The quadroons are almost entirely white; from their skin no one could detect their origin; nay, many of them have as fair a complexion as many of the haughty Créole females. Such of them as frequent these balls are free. Formerly they were known by their black hair and eyes, but at present there are completely fair quadroons male and female. Still, however, the strongest prejudice reigns against them because of their black blood, and the white ladies maintain, or affect to maintain the most violent aversion to them.''

These quadroon women competed with the "white Créole" ladies for their men's attention, affection, and in some cases final allegiance. They were the mistresses of the Créole men and often the mothers of their children. They constituted a separate society from either the white or the black worlds, i.e., they and their children.

It is a certainty that countless children of these quadroon mistresses and of other "gens de couleur" became assimilated into the white world. They and their descendants became members of the white society, and not of the black or Negroid.

After the Reconstruction Era, the prejudice against the Negro race as a whole began to gather momentum in the South. The Jim Crow policies were enforced, and to be black was to be enslaved once more; but this time in a more insidious manner.

There was suddenly no such person as "a free person of color," if indeed there ever had been, for the whites considered them to be black and the blacks considered them to be white. They were, however, told to sit in the "for colored only" sections along with those of "pure" black ancestry, and to adhere to all other Jim Crow policies concerning Negroes.

This "teint" (old French for color or taint) or "taint" limited the freedom of the "gens de couleur" as perhaps never before. The limitations of segregation were to be avoided if at all possible, and the only way to escape the legalized prejudice was either to leave the South or to "pass over the color line," (cross it and live as a Caucasian). Before World War II, "passing" was infinitely more desirable than leaving the South.

It is understandable why members of and even entire families "passed" over into the free white world of New Orleans and of the South. It is equally easy to understand why members of some of New Orleans' oldest families, some of whom claim lineage with the City's "Créole History," also deny that such a person as a "Créole of Color" ever existed.

Most Old-Guard New Orleanians declare that the only true definition of a Créole is the one that states: A "Créole is a person born in the colonies of pure Spanish and pure French parentage, a Caucasian," thereby asserting that "Créole of Color" is a contradiction of terms.

It may be absolutely true in many cases that the Créoles in some New Orleans family trees were all Caucasians, but it is also true that there were Créoles with Negro ancestors, Créoles of Color from the West Indies, containing members from both sides of the color line.

There are those members who recall old family history and stories, those who know "who was who, and what is what." Some know and tell tales. Others know and do not tell.

Antoine Meffre Rouzan, 1833
Portrait by Eugene Deveria
From the Collections of Louisiana State Museum
Monsieur Rouzan, a Créole of Color, married a white plantation owner's daughter. The couple soon afterward moved to Paris, France where they set up their household. Some of their children returned to New Orleans and re-established their family's history in the city.

Three Women of Fashion
Watercolor by M. Marquis, 1867
From the Collections of Louisiana State Museum

History

Hernando De Soto, a Spaniard, discovered the Mississippi River in 1541. La Salle explored the river well over one hundred years later, when plans were formulated to establish a French Empire that would stretch the length of the Mississippi from French Canada to the Gulf of Mexico.

Pierre Le Moyne d'Iberville, a French Naval officer born in Canada, was sent by France to colonize Louisiana in 1697, and in 1699 he visited the site where New Orleans was eventually built. But it was Jean Baptiste Le Moyne d'Bienville who founded the city of Nouvelle Orleans, named in honor of the Duke of Orleans, His Royal Highness, the Regent of France, in 1718.

The 1712 census of the area from Mobile, Alabama to New Orleans, and up river to Natchez, Mississippi, was 342 men.

"The Company of the West" was formed in France in 1715 and was headed by John Law. Law began an elaborate campaign to encourage Frenchmen to go to the colony of Louisiana. He began his propaganda much earlier in Germany. Pamphlets were distributed stating, among other fantastic claims, "the land is filled with gold, silver, and copper and lead mines. If one wishes to hunt for mines, he need only go into the country of the Natchitoches (an Indian tribe). There he will surely draw pieces of silver cut out of the earth."

In 1722 most of the colonists deported from France to Louisiana were criminals and deserters of one sort or another. But the King also deported many aristocrats and "citizens of quality and distinction." Certain of these people had requested to travel to New Orleans so as to escape imprisonment in the Bastille or elsewhere. Others were "highly placed men." These men and their wives journeyed to the New World in the name of their King and their country.

By 1723, the territory was peopled with civil and military officials — trappers, soldiers, redemptioners, merchants, and slaves. The slaves were either imported directly from Africa or from the French possessions in the West Indies. And, there were also the "Esclaves Naturels" who were the Indian prisoners of war.

The *Code Noir* was drawn up in 1724 to control the Negroes on the island of Santo Domingo. Governor Bienville announced that the same laws would apply to Louisiana with the added provisions that Jews were to be expelled from the colony, under penalty of confiscating their property and also imprisonment. The Catholic faith would be established as the State faith.

Eighty-eight young women, accompanied by nuns, were sent from France in 1728 with the sole intention of being "married off." Each girl brought with her "a dower" packed into a small case that held "two pairs of coats, two shirts and undershirts, six head-dresses, and additional furnishings." Within three months, thirty-one of the "Casket Girls" had found husbands.

A view of New Orleans was given by Sister Madline Hachard De Saint-Stanislas when writing to her father in 1728. The letter describes the city as a "modest though enjoyable settlement." She found reason to laud the area for its excellent food and its abundance of seafoods and wild game. She did, however, remark on the negative aspects, most notably the mosquitoes and the females of the city. "The women are careless of their salvation, but not of their vanity. Everyone here has luxuries, all of an equal magnificence. The greater part of them eat hominy but are dressed in velvet or damask, trimmed with ribbons. They use powder and rouge to hide the wrinkles on their faces, and wear beauty-spots. The devil has a vast empire here, but that only strengthens our hope of destroying it, God willing."

"The Company of the West" gave up its charter in 1731 after fourteen years, and though it was a financial failure, it succeeded in further populating the vast new territory. Within ten years the population of New Orleans had increased seven times over.

The French first ruled New Orleans from 1718 until 1763, and by the time of French Governor Vaudreul's rule, which extended from the year 1743 until 1753, the city had become a somewhat sophisticated and gay social center.

On February 6, 1763, Louisiana was ceded to Spain by the Treaty of Paris. That rule continued until November 30, 1803 when France again took possession of the colony from Spain. December 20th, twenty days later, Claiborne and General Wilkinson took possession of Louisiana in the name of the United States.

From the earliest days, New Orleans had its "Free People of Color," i.e., children fathered by Frenchmen and Spaniards and born of black slave women. Mulattoes were born almost before any white women arrived in the Louisiana territory. Children were also born of unions between Indian women and the French and Spanish soldiers, explorers, and adventurers. The melding began early in the history of the Latin colony.

The white fathers, by way of protecting their own children, sometimes set the mothers free so that the children would be born free. These offspring and their mothers, plus the many "Free Men and Free Women" who came from the West Indian Islands soon created a society of their own. This was a society of Mulattoes, Quadroons, Octaroons, the Griffes (*Mulatto*: a child of a Negro and a Caucasian; *Quadroon*: the child of a Mulatto and a Caucasian, a person having one-fourth Negro blood; *Octaroon*: the child of a Caucasion and a Quadroon, one-eighth Negro blood [however, the form is non-etymological, from Latin Octo, eight and from Quadroon, the suffix -oon]; *Griffe*: the child of a Mulatto and a Negro, three-fourths Negro blood), and Half-breeds (the child of an American Indian and a Caucasian).

There were "pure white" Créoles, men and women born of Caucasian French and Spanish colonists who had ventured to the new world, met and mated. Their child born in the colonies was dubbed a "Créole." Their customs, mores and language became known as "Créole."

When the "pure white" Créole mated with Negroes, mulattoes and quadroons in New Orleans, Cuba, Guadeloupe, Haiti, or any of the other French/Spanish ruled islands in the Caribbean, another hybrid came into existence, one who also spoke the patois, while adding his own variations. These also lived by the Créole codes and customs, adding unique flavorings to those rituals and foods, music and religion.

This hybrid was known as "Free Women of Color" and as "Free Men of Color," or as they were known in French, "Gens de Couleur Libre." Some of the Gens de Couleur eventually owned property, plantations and slaves as well, and it was as typical for these moneyed people to send their offspring to France to be educated as it was for the "white Créoles" to sent theirs. After the War between the States, the custom declined along with the wealth of the area and the customs of the Créoles. By the early 1800's, the Free Men of Color were so numerous they were able to form a regiment of their own, and they fought against the British in the Battle of New Orleans at Chalmette, Louisiana in 1815.

In 1728, during Spanish Governor Galvez's rule, a prohibition against the further importation of Negro slaves from Martinique was instituted ". . . as these Negroes are too much given to Vood[oo]ism, and make the lives of the citizens unsafe." There was a large influx of slaves and Créoles from other Caribbean Islands from 1791 to 1810. "Refugees" swarmed into the city, fleeing the slave insurrection in Santo Domingo. They also came from Cuba, Guadeloupe, Haiti, and other islands in the West Indies when the war against Napoleon exposed them to Spanish and British anti-French feelings.

Within a five-year period, over 8,000 "refugees" arrived, only one-third of whom were whites, the majority being free "Gens de Couleur" and slaves. These West Indians deepened the Voodoo cult within Louisiana and, most especially, in New Orleans.

Before this migration, in 1790, New Orleans was a city of only eight thousand, and yet fifteen hundred of these citizens were unmarried women of color. The French and Spanish "ladies" seem to have instituted the prohibitions and ordinances of 1788 that were meant to control the "Free Women of Color." Under Governor Miro, laws were passed that stated that only tignons (madras handkerchiefs tied around the head) were to be used as head coverings, and that it would be treated as "an evidence of misconduct if one of

Lake Pontchartrain, 1890
Photograph by George Francois Mugnier
From the Collections of Louisiana State Museum

these women walks abroad in silk, jewels or plumes" — that they would be "liable for punishment."

The warning from the Latin White Créole society was clear. These ladies of color were to remain in the background. But these women were not to be subdued. They blossomed into the famous and infamous quadroon caste of New Orleans, around whom the "Quadroon Ball" fame arose and flourished. Their unique qualities and beauty became immortalized.

The Quadroon Balls were attended only by the young and as yet "unchosen free women of color and by the white Créole gentlemen who were seeking to form an alliance with one of the young quadroon girls. These women were not prostitutes, but educated to be chaste and Catholic. They regarded their relationships with the Créole gentleman as marriages.

There were "little houses" on the edge of town near the Ramparts (today called Rampart Street) where the gentlemen kept their quadroon mistresses. Henceforth, the women were considered "Placée." Ensconced with their gen-

Praline Seller, 1885
Photograph by George Francois Mugnier
From the Collections of Louisiana State Museum

Créoles of New Orleans

Congo Square, 1890
Photograph by George Francois Mugnier
From the Collections of Louisiana State Museum

tlemen, the children of these alliances were free people of color. The property (the little house) belonged to the woman. She usually took the man's name and also gave his name to the children of the union.

The gentlemen, almost without exception, legally married convent-bred, Ursuline educated white Créole girls, and many of the quadroon mistresses, when abandoned after these church weddings, did themselves marry free men of color. Some never married, and almost never did a quadroon marry a man of darker skin. Too, some were never put aside or abandoned, even after her gentleman's "other marriage."

The best of the Quadroon Balls was held in the old Orleans Theatre and Ballroom, situated just behind St. Louis Cathedral on Orleans Street. In this theatre the Balls gained mythic fame, but they declined in popularity along with much of the glamour of old New Orleans with the advent of the War Between the States.

Later, this building became the Convent of the Sisters of the Holy Family, an order of Negro nuns. Today it is the site of a hotel.

The "Gens de Couleur" arriving in 1791 through 1809 were a highly sophisticated group, and they brought with them their patois, their culture and cults, their charms, and spices for food and for life.

A company of actors from Cap Français came and eventually opened its own theatre on St. Peter Street in 1791, becoming the first professional theatrical troupe to perform in the state of Louisiana. Louis Tabary and his group of "singing actors" performed exclusively in French. Not until the late 1800's were American and German theatres opened.

The colorful emigrés from the Caribbean formed a society of their own and were a force in the life of the city. Some opened schools, and others taught dancing and music.

In the early 1840's two literary journals were published by Créoles of Color, "L'Album Litteraire des Jeunes Gens, Amateur de Litterature" and "Les Cenelles," Editor, Armand Lanusse. They also established two newspapers in the 1860's, "L'Union" which was printed from 1862 through the year of 1864 and "La Tribune de la Nouvelle Orleans," a daily which was published from 1864-1869.

Les Cenelles, "Holly Berries," contained eighty-five poems, each of which was penned by gens de couleur who were french speaking and french educated. The authors included: Armand Lanusse, editor; Camille Thierry; P. Dalcour; B. Valcour; M.F. Liotau, and Michel St. Pierre.

Below is a poem by Lanusse entitled Le Songe, in English "The Dream."

Le Songe
A Mademoiselle C***

Poète à l'âme usée,
De tout trouble ennemi,
Sur ma lyre brisée
Je m'étais endormi.

Mais hier dans un songe
Un ami m'apparrut,
Disant: "Poète, Songe
A payer ton tribut."

De tout barde créole
Une jeune beauté
Réclame un chant frivole
Ou triste à volonté.

Et, dans mon âme émue
Répandant un parfum,
Une fée à ma vue
Offrit un riche album.

Ma fibre poétique
Avec arduer battit,
D'une voix angélique
Le fée alors me dit:

"Mon nom est C***
Dormeur, réveille-toi;
Je suis jeune et jolie,
Il faut chanter pour moi."

Plein d'un nouveau délire,
Soudain je m'éveillai;
Puis, remontant ma lyre,
Pour elle je chantai.

A free translation of "The Dream" of Mademoiselle C***

I am a poet with a worn spirit,
It is a most disquieting enemy,
On my broken lyre
I have been asleep.

But, yesterday in a dream
A friendly apparition appeared
Saying: "Poet, you must dream
To pay your tribute."

From all créole bards
A young beauty
Demands that you sing
Of frivolity or sadness at will.

And my soul moved
Pouring forth a perfume,
A fairy came into my life
Offering a rich album.

My poetic feelings were
Filled with throbbing ardor,
With the voice of an angel
The fairy then said to me:

"My name is C***
You were sleeping, I will awaken you;
I am young and pretty,
You must sing for me."

Full of a new ecstasy
I suddenly awakened;
Then, taking up my lyre again,
For her I shall sing.

Créoles of New Orleans

A French "patois" (patois: any regional French dialect) was spoken by most of the newcomers, though some did speak a "true Parisien." The slaves spoke a dialect reflecting the Créole French spoken by their masters. They also imitated the music and dances of their owners.

The slaves of the Caribbean, however, had their own dances. Some were variations on dances originating in Africa. Most had their roots in religion.

"La danse nègre est venue avec ceux d'Afrique à Santo Domingue, et pour cette raison même elle est commune à ceux qui sont nés dans la colonie et qui la pratiquent presque en naissant: On l'y appelle Calenda.

Le plus court de ces tambours est nommé Bamboula, attendu qu'll est formé qualquefois d'un très gros bambou.

Une autre danse nègre, à Saint-Domingue, qui est aussi d'origine Africaine, c'est Le Chica, nommé simplement Calenda aux Iles du Vent, Congo à Cayenne, Fandangue en Espagne, etc. Cette danse a un air qui lui est spécialement consacré et où la mesure est fortement marquée.

La Calenda et Le Chica ne sont pas le seules danses venues d'Afrique dans la colonie. Il en est une autre que l'on y connîit depuis longtemps, principalement dans la partie occidentale, et qui porte le nom de vaudou."

The Negroes who came from Africa to Santo Domingo brought their dances with them, and for that same reason it is common also to those born in the colonies and they practice them nearly from their birth.

The shortest one on the drum is called the Bamboula, formed from rhythmic beatings on bamboo.

View of St. Louis Cathedral, mid 1800's.
by A. Magny
From the Collections of Louisiana State Museum

Another Negro dance in Santo Domingo, originating in Africa, is Le Chica, called simply Calenda in the windward islands from the Congo to Cayenne, and the Fandango in Spain. That dance has an especially strong beat.

The Calenda and the Chica are not the only dances to come from Africa into the colonies. Another one that has been known for a long time, principally in the Western part of Africa is named the Vaudaux, or Voodoo.

While "Vaudaux" was danced and practiced as a cult in the West Indies before the 1800's, not until the Créoles of Color and their slaves brought the ritual to Louisiana did it have the impact that it eventually attained. (Voodoo: A religious cult of African Negroes of Haiti characterized by a belief in sorcery, fetishes and rituals in which participants communicate by trance with ancestors, Saints or animistic deities. 2. A charm, fetish, spell, or curse believed by adherents of this cult to hold magic power.)

By 1825, New Orleans had become a civilized "Créole City." Opera, French theatre, balls, music, and gambling flourished.

In the early 1800's the population was less than ten thousand. By 1822 the census counted more than forty thousand.

New Orleans was poorly defended during the War Between the States, and after a five day seige fought at Forts Jackson and St. Philip on the River, the city surrendered April 20, 1862, and General Benjamin Butler assumed command of the city.

On May 11, 1864, the Constitution of Louisiana was amended and slavery was abolished. The years between 1865 and 1877 brought much racial and political strife. There were countless riots between whites and blacks.

Bird's Eye View of New Orleans, 1852
by Muller
From the Collections of Louisiana State Museum

Créoles of New Orleans

Oscar J. Dunn, the Lieutenant-Governor of Louisiana during Henry Clay Warmouth's reconstruction administration was a mulatto, as was Lieutenant-Governor "Pinkey" Pinchback who became the acting Governor in the year 1873.

"The Golden Age" in Louisiana existed in the years between 1830 and 1860, when the plantation system was at its peak and the steamboat commerce brought and carried goods to and from the rest of the world and laid wealth at New Orleans' doorstep. In those years slaves labored and reaped great wealth for their masters. Gambling, Mardi Gras, balls, fine restaurants, theatres, and opera all flourished. Prosperity reigned.

The War Between the States ended this Golden Era for New Orleans as it ended the prosperity of most of the South. The large plantations no longer had slaves to work their enormous land holdings, and the emergence of the railroads superseded the commercial use of the Mississippi River. Most of the old ways were replaced by more expedient methods and means. The Americanization of New Orleans began. Large numbers of Sicilians began arriving in 1880. The Americans and new emigrés eventually outnumbered and overpowered the influence of the Créoles of the city. In 1900, the population was 287,104.

and the major celebration, Mardi Gras with its attending balls and parades, continues to hold sway. Though in the more subtle acts of daily living many of the "Créole" and "Latin" ways are consistently losing ground, much of New Orleans' famous hospitality, food, exotic gaiety and unique charm still remains.

Souvenir de la Nouvelle Orleans, 1852
From the Collections of Louisiana State Museum

A View of Esplanade Avenue, 1890
Photograph by George Francois Mugnier
From the Collections of Louisiana State Museum

The Mississippi River
New Orleans is not only below the flood level of the Mississippi River, but more than one half of its flat surface is below storm level of its "backyard," Lake Pontchartrain.
There is approximately five feet of rain each year, all of which must be pumped off the land and back into the Lake, the River and assorted canals (such as the London Avenue Canal). There is no outward flow through gravitation.
The port of New Orleans has over twenty-five miles of public and private docks.

Esplanade Avenue

The Créole section of New Orleans is also in the seventh ward. The boundaries of the ward are the Mississippi River, Elysian Fields, Esplanade Avenue, and Lake Pontchartrain. Residents of "The Créole Section" will tell you that the boundaries of the neighborhood are St. Claude, Elysian Fields, Esplanade Avenue, and Dillard University, or "maybe a few blocks just behind Dillard toward the lake."

What Is A Créole?

Créole?
Free men and women of color

My auntee was in her 90's when she died a fine
Looking woman . . . Secret? Don't worry about nuthin'
You die. . . .
Everybody dies
God takes French
Everybody away
Don't worry!!

Créole?
French I'm sure.

What Is A Créole?

The writer, Lyle Saxon, was born in Baton Rouge and came to New Orleans just before World War I. He worked as a newspaper reporter for the New Orleans Item and the Times Picayune and wrote many wonderful books about the city.

Saxon was "personally dedicated to the preservation and the restoration of the Vieux Carré." In his book *Fabulous New Orleans,* he included the following: "The Créole is not of colored blood. Locally the word means French or Spanish descent, or of a mixed descent, French and Spanish. The Créole was the child of European parents born in a French or Spanish colony. The New Orleans Créole is our finest product. The women are lovely, and the men are brave. They have charming manners. They are exclusive; they are clannish; they keep to themselves. Can anyone blame them? They have their own language, their own society, and their own customs. What language do they speak? They spoke and still speak a pure French. The reason the word "Créole" has been so often misunderstood is because their slaves spoke a Créole dialect bearing about the same relation to pure French as our Southern Negro talk bears to English purely spoken."

This book was published in 1928.

St. Bernard Avenue
No one disputes that St. Bernard Avenue runs through the center of the 7th ward . . . the Créole Section.

*The Mason's Hall "Etoile Polaire" (North Star)
on St. Claude near Esplanade Ave.
Etoile Number 1 was built in 1840 for the Worshipful Polar
Star Lodge Number 1. This chapter of the Louisiana Masonic
Community was chartered by the State Legislature, March
18, 1816. Lodge members have included Jean La Mothe, William Charles Claiborne (first governor of the State of
Louisiana), and De Marigny, among others.*

*Old light post on St. Bernard Avenue
near St. Claude Avenue*

From A Conversation With Louis Joseph Saloy Sr.

"Certainly the Créole did exist. It wasn't white — the white folks *make* it white. All right? The definition of Créole is black people intermingling with whites, the Frenchmen and Spanish and so forth . . . O.K.? That's the Créoles amongst the Negroes in the city of New Orleans, the light complected Negroes. That's where it started from. . . . It's a mixture! You gotta have some black in you to be a Créole! But, the whites want to claim that everything is Créole. They wrong! It's not that way; never was that way. Créole is amongst Negroes . . . the fair complected. And they got black Créoles; they speak that language . . . *that* broken Cajun language.

Créoles of New Orleans

"Everybody in my family speaks French but me, cause I was — I was gone too much, never a chance to say nary nothin'. But the Créole is really Negroes! White people say Créole means . . . white! It don't work that way. Créole is Negroes that mingled with whites. . . . White men had colored women. That's what it really means . . . the offspring. . . . It don't mean a hundred percent, no! Like in my family . . . there were three brothers who came from France. Two brothers married white women and one married an octaroon. That's a mixed breed woman . . . that's *my* offspring! O.K.? But, that's still three brothers from France . . . the name Saloy . . . pronounced 'Sallwaa.' French!

"I mean these people is way out the way! Look! Hear the way this thing works. See my complexion? But, all my wives been black cause I got that in my heart. And that's where my feelins' is . . . because I got it in my blood. And it's as simple as that. And that's what happened back here in the seventh ward. Everybody is mixed. But, they more aggressive here than in the other wards — they all mechanics . . . meaning that they help one another . . . builders, bricklayers, this and that, and most the people around here got they start by helpin' one another.

"You want to build a house? They know you?! They come on Saturday, and Sunday, after they work all week! And they help you build a house. All you got to do is buy your own materials. Don't pay um or nothin'. Buy a couple of barrels of beer and have some red beans and rice or somethin like that, and they gonna build your house for you. . . . That's the tradition of the seventh ward . . . helpin' one another.

"'Do unto others as others gonna do unto you'. . . . I believe in that, that's my creed, O.K.? And I really believe it!

"And, they still help one another. You need somethin' done? You want somethin' done? You want to add a room?! Have a few drinks! Help out!

"People don't know like us, like the real seventh warders. Other people do, but they don't do like we came up and done.

"I done been everywhere. They ain't no place like New Orleans . . . no place.

"I got sons and daughters live up in Seattle. They beg me to come up there. They say it's pretty — they got sunshine! Can't see it — ain't no place like New Orleans. And I've been all through Europe — Marseilles, Lyon — you name it, Casablanca, Peru, Algiers, Orient, all them places in Africa; and I *know* there's no place like New Orleans. No food like here — no way. . . . Life is what you make it."

Créole house

The Castle

Mrs. Emily Trevigne lives in the "first gallery house on the block" now. She used to live right next door to "the castle" when she was growing up.

"Mr. Rudolpho, who was an Austrian, I'm sure, built the castle with the help of a colored gentleman from down here. Built it around 1921. I remember when he and his wife lived in one room with a sod floor. He added on to that little by little over the years until "the castle" was built. Oh! He built and built — built over the line of his property as a matter of fact.

"'Can't do that!' my father told him.

"Rudolpho said he *wasn't* over! But, he sure was! He was a greedy man. Built right up to our house, right on top of us. I could look outside my window and touch his bathtub! Greedy man! He *did* have to pay, cause he *was* over on our property line. That was a long, long time ago. Don't know who lives there now."

"You want the tempo of the seventh ward?! This is what you'd call your hard hat ward! We're noted for our tradesmen . . . bricklayers . . . carpenters . . . tile men . . . roofers . . . noted for they barbers too!"

Two "Mulatto Corps" were formed to fight the British in the defense of New Orleans in the War of 1812. Savary, a man of color from Santo Domingo who eventually attained the rank of Captain under General Andrew Jackson, was very successful in his efforts to raise a company of men of color, many of whom were refugees from the island, too. The command of this batallion was given to Major Daquin, of the 2nd Regiment of Militia, who was a white refugee from the island of Santo Domingo. Both Savary and Daquin had fought during the slave insurrection in Santo Domingo and had fled to Louisiana "on being overpowered by their enemies."

The second company was commanded by Major Lacoste. Michel Fortier, a native of New Orleans and a wealthy merchant, was appointed Colonel and took command of both of the corps, which numbered close to six hundred men.

On December 18, 1814, (before the Battle of New Orleans occurred on January 8, 1815) General Andrew Jackson reviewed his forces and the following address was read to "The Men of Color" by one of his aides: "Soldiers! I collected you to arms; I invited you to share in the perils and to divide the glory of your white countrymen. I expect much from you, for I was not uninformed of those qualities which must render you so formidable to an invading foe. I knew that you would endure hunger and thirst and all the hardships of war. I knew that you loved the land of your nativity, and that, like ourselves, you had to defend all that is most dear to man; but you surpass my hopes. I have found in you, united to those qualities, that noble enthusiasm which impels to great deeds. Soldiers! The President of the United States shall be informed of your conduct on the present occasion, and the voice of the Representation of the American Nation shall applaud your valor, as your General now praises your ardor. The enemy is near; his sails cover the lakes; but the brave are united; and if he finds us contending among ourselves, it will be for the prize of valor, and fame its noblest reward."

This highly complimentary address was met with disfavor among many who deemed it "bad policy to address them in terms which were not in accordance with the inferiority of their social position, and which might tend to raise hopes that could never be gratified." To those critics Jackson said: "The two corps of colored volunteers have not disappointed the hopes that were formed of their courage and perseverance in the performance of their duty. Majors Lacoste and Daquin who commanded them, have deserved well of their country."

What is a *Free Jack?*

The term *Free Jacks* was born at the Battle of New Orleans in 1815. A number of slaves fought under the command of General Andrew Jackson at Chalmette, Louisiana, located several miles below New Orleans on the Mississippi River's edge. The slaves fought so valiantly, that after the battle General Jackson granted each man his freedom.

Jackson signed a document for each slave, and as the story goes, he signed so many that the only truly legible words written on the page were the words *free* and the first five letters of the general's last name *Jacks.* And so, the term *Free Jacks* and not "free, signed, Jackson" was created.

A *Free Jack!*

Food And Hospitality

Minnie Coignet dishes up red beans for dinner.

In the mid-nineteenth century, Prince Achille Murat (Prince Royal of the Two Sicilies) visited New Orleans and made the following observation: "If there is little intellectual conversation, however, ample means are afforded for eating, playing, dancing, and making love."

Lavish hospitality in the form of delicious and unusual foods has been served up to citizens and visitors alike since the city began. It is still one of the siren calls for most visitors. The city abounds with cafes and restaurants that serve extraordinary food. There are also kitchens in homes in which favorite family recipes are discussed and devoured with gusto — "Daddy's gumbo!" . . . "Auntee's stuffed mirlitons!" . . . "Cousin's beans!" . . . "Mama's crawfish bisque!" Each family has a member who makes "the best" of each of the New Orleans favorites. Recipes are recited aloud to any guest who asks the cook. Recipes are dissected, compared and discussed endlessly, as are restaurants in which specific dishes considered to be essential to the local diet can be found "cooked to perfection," etc. — foods from oysters on the half shell, prized for perfect saltiness and served at the correct temperature, to gumbo, should it be prepared with sausage and seafood, chicken as well? Such questions are quite earnestly asked and answered time and time again. The city has long been preoccupied with the preparation and consumption of "quality" foods, much like France herself.

Circle Food Store in St. Bernard Market

In 1722, Father Charlevoix described a New Year's day turtle dinner: "This is certain, that the meat of that which I saw, was enough to satisfy ten persons who had good stomachs." Mark Twain, when served the local fish, pampano, declared that it was as "delicious as the less criminal forms of sin." And Thackeray, after tasting a New Orleans bouillabaisse said, "Better was never eaten at Marseilles, and not a headache in the morning, upon my word, only awoke with a sweet, refreshing thirst for claret and water." He added that New Orleanians live in "the city of the world where you can eat and drink the most and suffer the least."

A seemingly endless bounty of game meats — venison, wild turkey, partridge, woodcock, snipe, wild duck, and geese, as well as seafood, unsurpassed in flavor and variety, exotic spices, vegetables, and fruits, all provided in Louisiana — furnished cooks and chefs with quite a supply of foods with which to experiment.

Créole cuisine developed over the years and owes its development to the spicy seasonings of Spanish cooking, added to the subtle sauces of the French, combined with the native herbs of the Choctaw Indians; filé being most notably used in what has been called "The Elixer of Créole Life," commonly called "Gumbo."

Over the years native New Orleanians and Louisianians, both black and white, have added their distinctive touches, thereby further developing a unique American cuisine, "Créole Cuisine."

The following are a few local proverbs connected to food: "An empty sack cannot stand up." "Good coffee and the Protestant Religion were seldom if ever found together." "Créole coffee to be prepared perfectly must be . . . Noir comme le diable . . . Fort comme la mort . . . Doux comme l'amour . . . Chaud comme l'enfer!" ("Black as the devil, strong as death, sweet as love, hot as hell!"). "To prepare the perfect Créole salad dressing, a Spanish proverb is used: It takes four to make the perfect salad dressing. . . . A miser to pour the vinegar; a spendthrift to add the olive oil; a wise man to sprinkle the salt and pepper; and a madcap to mix and stir the ingredients."

The seasonings used in Créole cooking are distinctive; however, there is another essential ingredient. It is a heavy black iron skillet or pot in which to sauté the melange of spices and herbs. The combination creates the magic.

One must begin by "creating a roux." This is done by using one tablespoon of white flour to each tablespoon of hot oil or lard, blending the two, then slowly, very slowly, browning the flour in the magic iron pot placed over a medium low flame. After the perfect brownness has been achieved, a combination of seasonings are added, sautéed until the onions (a must) are transparent, then water and or wine is added to make "the gravy" or sauce. Seasonings in various combinations include green, red, black, cayenne, and banana peppers, garlic, yellow onions, shallots, scallions, bay leaf, thyme, basil, celery, parsley and filé (ground sassafras root bark).

Of course using the foods of the region in preparing New Orleans dishes is most desirable, however a tasty facsimile can be concocted using one's own imagination in selecting alternatives. But, whenever possible, use crawfish, oysters, shrimp, pampano, flounder, red fish, cowan, frog legs, and other seafood from Louisiana waters and from the Gulf of Mexico just off the coast of Louisiana. Ideally, the soft-shell, hard-shell and buster crabs should be from Lake Pontchartrain and its connecting waterways; cowan from the marshes and bayous, yams, rice, cane syrup, and sugar from South Louisiana; Louisiana-made sausages in Jambalaya and beans; citrus from Plaquemines Parish, just south of New Orleans; and Créole tomatoes, peppers, mirlitons, and herbs grown in a New Orleans back yard. And it is also said that in order to prepare the perfect cup of chicory laden Créole coffee and cook the perfect roux gravy, one needs to use Mississippi River water as it passes New Orleans' front door.

As to the hospitality of the city and her Créoles, you can be sure that there is always a pot of coffee warming on one of the back burners and a large pot of gumbo or red beans or white beans simmering alongside the colander of cooked rice. "Are you hungry? How 'bout a cup of coffee, cher?" Those are two of the first questions you will be asked upon entering a home. The next question will most likely be, "Comment sa va?" ("How does it go with you?").

The attitude of hospitality was summed up by Maude Randolph. "Do unto others as you would have others do unto you. That's the Golden Rule my generation was taught. . . . And so we shared. . . . If you have a pot of beans, share it and enjoy it!"

The city's unique cuisine and history of gracious hospitality have been created by all of her exotic citizens, a melange that began with a heaping measure of French, Spanish and black, a pinch of Indian, then later by adding a dash of Anglo-Saxon. The mixture has been stirred together, blended, cooked down very slowly, and is served up as the spicy dish called "Créole."

The I-10 Expressway replaced an avenue of live oak trees that once lined the neutral ground of N. Claiborne Avenue.

What Is A Créole?
Herbert Jones

T he Cowan Man . . . the Vegetable Man . . . the Salesman. . . .
"People stand like bees around a hive watchin' me cut the cowan in
pieces! I've been 29 years right around this circle." He points directly
at the spot a block away where the St. Bernard circle was, the circle that was
in front of the "Circle Market" on St. Bernard Avenue and Claiborne Avenue.
"I was born 2 blocks down. Never been out of the city in my life. I lived next
door to our ex-mayor "Dutch" Morial. I have 9 children, 19 grandchildren
and 5 great-grandchildren, 11 nieces and nephews. I'm the salesman. Been
talkin' for a livin' all my life, since I was twelve. My daddy was a charcoal-man
. . . a nickel a bucket. He'd hit me on the head and say, "'Whatever you be,
be the *best* one!'

"See this cowan? Now, there are 7 types of meat in a cowan, and it must
be cooked with a strong gravy . . . plenty of thyme and bay leaf, garlic and
onion, lots of seasonings, and you gotta have potato salad with it!" The crowd
gathered around repeats, "Potato salad! Yeah!"

"7 types of meat! Fish, chicken, stew meat, beef. . . ." His voice trails
off. "The male's shell is flat. The female's shell is round. Now, the eggs are
soft. They never get hard. You bust 'um in the gravy and eat 'um . . .
Ummm! See these jaws?! No teeth. . . . But! Jaws! That's it! Strong! To
make him let go, you got to light a fire behind him, and he'll open his mouth
and let go . . . a big fire with a paper!

"The cowan is a mud turtle, a snappin' turtle, and you find it in marshes
out near Laplace, Venice . . . Got to go far now. It's $1.75 a pound. This
one is $24.50. Should have seen the cowan last week. Big! Yeah! It's a Créole
delicacy. You ever eat it? Nothin' like sea turtle, nothin'! Delicious!"

The crowd around repeats and mutters, "*Oh*, yeah!"

Herbert Jones selling his wares

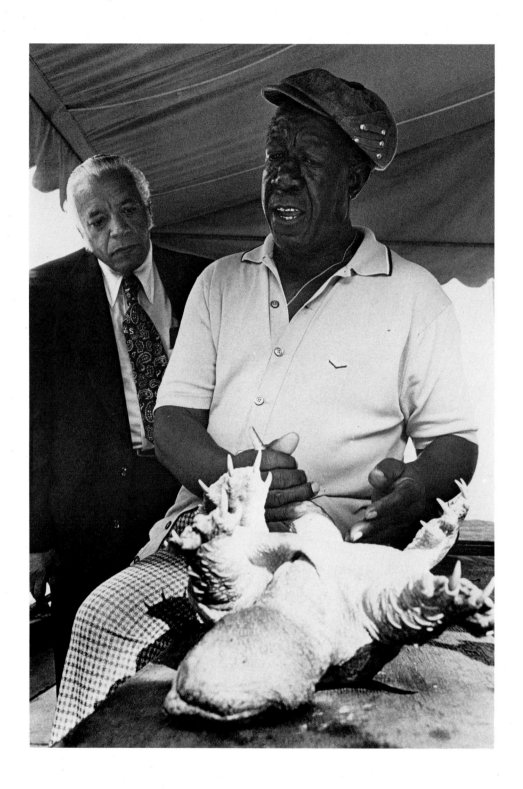

A "Cowan"
In 1722 Father Charlevoix described a New Year's Day Turtle dinner: "This is certain, that the meat of that which I saw was enough to satisfy ten persons who had good stomachs."
Turtle and Frog were everyday fare in old New Orleans, as were all types of wild game, including Venison, Wild Turkey, Partridge, Quail, Woodcock, Snipe, Wild Duck and Geese.

Bacheman's Butcher Shop
Tyrone, Wayne and Walter Bacheman; Joseph Pratts and Ricardo Neves.
"The best hot sausage in the city of New Orleans. My sister just took 30 pounds back to West Los Angeles, 'the other Créole section' . . . where many expatriates of the seventh ward live."

If you're "home" visiting in the Créole section you're probably from West Los Angeles, a sort of Créole home-away-from-home for the countless expatriates who fled the south and its stultifying limitations in the 1940's and 50's. You were baptized Catholic, probably at Corpus Christi Church, but perhaps at Epiphany Church. Your family is filled with stories about the relatives, great and near great, who are passé blanc — passing for white. They are from your family; had the same black great grandmother as you or the same white grandmother as you. You most probably have a French surname if you're a man; your maiden name was French if you're a woman, perhaps your first name, too. The older members of your family can still speak "un peu Français" (a little French), and all of their parents spoke nothing but French in the home. Your skin "couleur" will range from "pure" white to café au lait. How

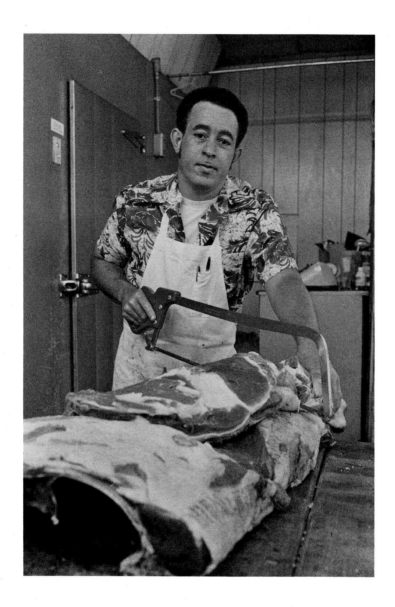

dark or how light depends on how much cream you take in your café. Your eyes might be brown, but chances are they are hazel . . . or blue . . . or grey. . . .

As a Créole baby, when you were born you had blue blue eyes and red hair, and as a Créole, "in ten months it'll all be gone!" Your eyes are now hazel and your hair is chatain — brown.

Perhaps some of your family traveled from Haiti to New Orleans in 1719 from France or directly to New Orleans . . . or. . . .

Your mere-mere said "Pas connais!" and not "Je ne connais pas!" for "I don't know or understand." Your father, grandfather, uncles, and brothers belonged to the Autocrat Club. You're a Créole?! But what is a Créole?

Crawfish! Crayfish! Mud-Bugs! Devine!

Byron Shorter
Cook at Bert's Peacock Room Bar and Restaurant

I t's dark, and cool and red.
No hurry at all
Pleasant and seductive and delicious
Better
More than your mama ever "prepared"
Dark red gravy and "creamed" potatoes fresh
Pork chops smothered
Vegetables
Strange palate developed in New Orleans
But, canned spinach tastes ever so much better than
Fresh cooked
Didn't I see you downtown the other day at the
Inauguration?
Naw!
The inauguration was at noon
I never get up before one. . . .

Religion

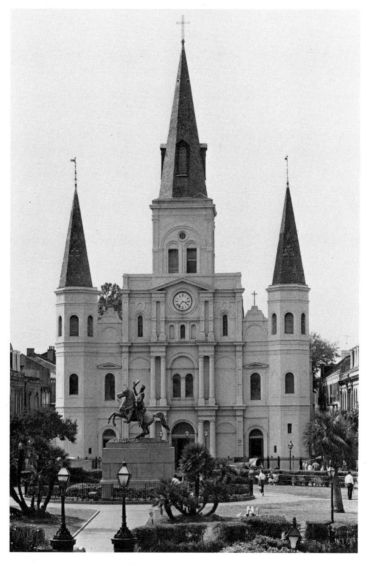

St. Louis Cathedral

New Orleans is a Latin city. From the beginning, when it was under
French and Spanish domination, the Roman Catholic Church domi-
nated the spiritual lives of its citizens. Much later in the city's history,
the Americans took over its rule, and the "Yankees" came to settle. The Protestant faith began making inroads; however, the influence and dominance has
remained that of the Catholic faith. In 1724, Catholicism was adopted as the
State faith.

Capuchin priests began educating the boys of the colony even before the
Ursuline nuns (founded in about 1537, the order dedicated to the education
of girls) opened a school for girls in 1727.

The Ursulines of Rouen were contracted through Father Beaubois, a
Jesuit priest in New Orleans, to come and establish an Ursuline convent. It
was founded in 1727 under the auspices of King Louis XV. The convent

building was completed in 1734 and today is still standing and considered to be the oldest structure in the entire Mississippi Valley.

Eight nuns, two postulants and a black servant constituted the first group; however, two nuns and one postulant soon returned to France, giving as one reason for their departure, "an unsuitable climate." The remaining nuns worked tirelessly, for they, in addition to their teaching duties, also maintained an orphanage and until 1770 were in charge of the Hospital.

In 1794 the present St. Louis Cathedral was erected on the site where the first Catholic Church stood. Here, countless citizens have been baptized, married, had burial services, and later, Masses said, all for the redemption of their "Immortal Souls."

Members of the Catholic hierarchy owned slaves, and since there were no objections raised by ecclesiastical authority, laymen logically determined that slave ownership was actually favored.

Most of the Catholic hierarchy and most of the lower clergy in America during the early days were French. The majority of slave owners in the Louisiana territory were French Catholics, and therefore their slaves came under the influence of the culture if not the direct influence of the Roman Catholic Church. The original black Catholics in this country were slaves, though after the emancipation many left to join newly-found Negro Protestant Churches.

Between World War I and II, the rate of conversions throughout the country was steady but small, despite the efforts of the Josephite Fathers and the Society of the Divine Word (who are pledged to work in black parishes), and also the all-black Sisterhoods — The Oblate Sisters of Providence, the Handmaids of Mary and the Sisters of the Holy Family.

The Sisters of the Blessed Sacrament, founded by Mother Katherine Drexel, a member of a wealthy Philadelphia family, was dedicated to work among the Negroes, though its members have been largely white. These Sisters of the Blessed Sacrament established Xavier University in New Orleans in 1891, which is the only Catholic Institution of higher learning with a predominantly Negro student body.

The black Catholic in America has always been rare and in 1973 was counted at approximately 800,000. Today fewer than 200 black priests are in the American clergy, and one-half of them are members of the Society of the Divine Word, an order that opened a special seminary for black candidates in Bay St. Louis, Mississippi in 1920. (Bay St. Louis is situated approximately 65 miles east of New Orleans on the Gulf Coast.)

Two of the Bay St. Louis graduates have been named Bishops: Bishop Joseph Bowers serves in Ghana, Bishop Harold Perry serves as the Auxiliary of the Archdiocese of New Orleans.

Today most of the Negro population in New Orleans belong to the Baptist and Methodist Churches, though there are still many Catholics.

The first Protestant Church, the Episcopalian Christ's Church was built in the city in 1816.

Denominations include: Presbyterian, Jewish, Lutheran, Christian Science, Adventists, American Old Catholic, Assembly of God, Church of Christ, Church of God, Church of the Nazarene, Disciples of Christ, Greek, Latter Day Saints, Rosicrucian, Theosophical Society, Unitarian and Unity, as well as many cult-like churches established by self-appointed leaders.

St. Rose of Lima

"When you were about ten years old, if they thought you could make it you went to St. Rose of Lima School."

"Make it?"

"Pass for white! Well, if they thought you could 'make it' they sent you to St. Rose of Lima School, and if you were too dark to pass and were just an ordinary Créole, why then you went to Corpus Christi School with all the other Créoles."

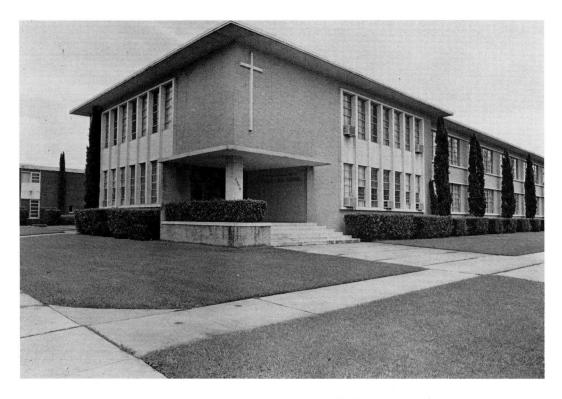

St. Augustine High Schol

St. Augustine High School opened its doors in the Fall of 1951. The first class graduated in 1955. Before "St. Aug" "there was no Catholic high school for young black men in New Orleans. A limited number could be accepted at Xavier Prep High School, which at that time was co-ed."

The alumni includes: Warren Bell, Sidney Barthelemy, Hank Braden, Trevor Bryan, Keith Butler, Louis Charbonnet, Fernell Chatman, Sherman Copelin, Charles Cotton, Ed Martin, Dwight Ott, Tom Perkins, Ronald Ruiz, Paul Valteau, James Buchanan Borders IV, Harold Sylvester, Vernel Bagneris, Anthony Barthelemy, Vaughn Glapion, Michael Williams, Nolan Marshall, Jr. Other notables include: Dwight McKenna, Keith Ferdinand, Michael Darnell, Dennis Bagneris and Michael Bagneris. Father Joseph Verrett is currently the principal.

A plaque in the hall near the front door reads, "It is the work of the Catholic School to equip man to know himself, his dignity, his potential, his world and his Creator."

Dillard University, built in the 1930's on Gentilly Boulevard.
The original school, Straight University, was
situated on Esplanade Avenue.

Dillard University opened in 1935, formed by a merger of New Orleans University, founded in 1869 by the Freedmen's Bureau for the Higher Education of Negroes, and Straight University, founded by the American Missionary Society of New York. The University, situated on a 63 acre campus, is supported by the Congregational and Methodist Churches and through private endowments and gives baccalaureate degrees in education, the humanities, the natural sciences, the social sciences, nursing, and the allied arts. Flint Goodrich Hospital is a unit of the University.

Corpus Christi Church founded in 1916.

The Coignets

O n Saturday, March 18, 1978 the Alfred J. Coignet Sr.'s celebrated the renewal of their wedding vows at Corpus Christi Church on St. Bernard Avenue. The celebration was held on the sixtieth anniversary of their marriage. Their four sons and one daughter, their grandchildren and great-grandchildren gathered to honor them.

Alfred J. Coignet Sr. was born in Napoleonville, Louisiana on February 17, 1894, and his wife, Minnie Martin, was born on December 5, 1895 in St. James Parish. They met at the wedding of Mr. Coignet's sister, Rezia Coignet, and Minnie Martin's brother, Aladin Martin. Immediately after their marriage in March of 1918, they moved to New Orleans and into the seventh ward, where they have remained.

"Sixty years! Alfred we made it! Thank God for that!"

1918 to 1978 . . . sixty years to settle in, settle down, merge and converge, conjoin, return to, return through, identify with, because of, through and beyond. Children. The family. Children.

The act of existing because of two, a particular two . . . two-some . . . couple . . . pair . . . duo . . . man and woman. Not group nor neighborhood, city nor house, flock nor tribe . . . but, two! The beginning . . . always a new beginning.

Alfred C. Coignet and Minnie Martin Coignet

*Howard Coignet, Andrew Coignet, Dorothy Coignet Stanley, Alfred Coignet, Jr.,
Linus Coignet, Sr. (seated) Alfred C. Coignet and Minnie Martin Coignet.*

Créoles of New Orleans

Coignet Family
Anthony Coignet, Rhonda Coignet, Elaine Coignet Ker, Jackie Coignet, Mavis Coignet,
Howard Coignet, Charmaine Coignet De Mouey, Andrew Coignet, Dorothy Coignet Stanley,
Alfred Coignet, Jr., Cynthia Stanley Davidson, Linus Coignet, Sr., Alcerdes Coignet, Linus
Coignet, Jr., Margaret Coignet, Theresa Coignet, Phillip De Mouey and Jason De Mouey. (left
to right seated) Thomas Stanley, Kerry Davidson, Jr., Maude Randolph, Mr. and Mrs. Alfred
Coignet, Sr., David Ker, Dawn Coignet, Vivian Coignet, and Eunice Coignet De Mouey.

The line. There exists the sureness that we, each of us, came from an
establishment of a relationship between a man and a woman . . . of a moment's duration or sixty years duration. Nevertheless, there is the undeniable
fact that we were begat, begun by only two . . . one man and one woman
giving unto us . . . for a moment's duration or sixty years duration . . . a
family.

How is it done — this living together for sixty years?

"I made the best of every day I've been here, and it wasn't always on
Easy Street you know!"
Both Minnie and Alfred Coignet look at one another, nod and laugh
together.
Alfred says that he has no regrets about life, and Minnie says that they've
made the best of it. Her only regret was that there wasn't a second girl child
(there are four sons and one daughter). Her greatest joy is "my family!"

Honky Time

A Honky:

A white employer who sits in front of the house in his car and honks for his employee.

Sure, I got a French name! But, *they* say I'm black!
See my skin? I don't *look* black . . .
But, they say I'm black, so I'm black!
What's black?
My great aunt was half white. . . .
My mama's strand never did break
My daddy's strand broke. His sister is so black she shines purple.

A Créole is black and French descent
Canadian French and Spanish
I'm French. Not Créole
Free women and men of color . . . mixed with whites. . . .

The men from this area were known for their fine brick-laying and plastering.
They were plumbers, too. . . .

The women . . . ?
No! They do not work
Not from the seventh ward
They stay home and take care of the fireside
That's the tradition. . . .

Cocks crow all day long in the seventh ward
Gravel streets suddenly turn into country-like dirt roads
Patches of weeds and vegetables grow side by side
Flowers and fig trees
Chickens er er er er errrrr!
Cockadoodle doo!

Créoles of New Orleans

Cockfights
Public cockfights were held on Sunday afternoons in the New Orleans of 1820. Bull fights were advertised in the newspapers of the day a few years later, and in 1890 Louisiana became one of the first states to legalize prize-fighting.

Créoles of New Orleans

The London Avenue Canal

Young men have been lured by her cool waters
To fish in her
To dive in and
To swim in her
Steeply angled concrete banks make her difficult to leave
Impossible for some

There was a young boy named for the River Shannon
Who found this Circe treacherous
Impossible to escape
Shannon had to be taken
From his parents
From this earth to be freed from
The London Avenue Canal

Cemeteries

There are those
More praised in death than life
More loved more revered
There are those
Whose adoration continues
A perpetuation of devotion
Those who hold a hope for a life more real after death
A deification. . . . An apotheosis

There are those
Saints who were sinners
Saints who were saints
Mothers and fathers, children and friends
More missed in death
Regrets and losses
Hope for what surely must come
Wishes and promises carved in marble
Regrets etched on death's door
Pledges of peace and perpetual care
In Golgotha

In St. Roch's Chapel

Though Mt. Olivet is the burial ground in the seventh ward, many residents who lived and live now in the seventh ward will have as their final place of rest the Campo Santo, St. Roch's Cemetery, which is located in the eighth ward.

Ex-votoes shine like grateful votive lights left by "clients" of Saint Roch's, who, in gratitude for the surcease of pain and newly won perfection of eye, foot or liver, leave replicas of the old afflicted body part with "thanks."

Yellow Fever

In 1796 General Victor Collot described the city as "an air always damp, stagnant waters and marshy grounds."

Abundant moisture remaining in the city, lack of underground sewers and sanitary conditions, plus stagnant waters and marshy grounds, all created ideal conditions for mosquitoes to breed copiously and helped create the Yellow Fever and Cholera epidemics that raged in the 1850's.

In *Gibson's Guide and Directory of the City*, 1838, Yellow Fever was referred to as an "acclimatizing fever." Indeed it was considered for a time as a "stranger's disease," for it seems that at least in 1853, very few native-born citizens of New Orleans were affected by the fever, although between June and October of that year it is estimated that the disease accounted for over 7,000 deaths, only 87 of which were New Orleanians.

As a method of allaying the "raging fevers" so prevalent in 1832, the height of the Cholera epidemic, a "scientific cure" was ordered by the city officials. They ordered the "burning of tar in the streets and the firing of cannons." This means of "purifying the atmosphere" was abandoned in 1853.

The "Mosquito Baire," a netting hung around the bed, was indispensable for sleeping, as the idea of screening the doors and the windows of the house was not immediately considered.

Even today determined efforts are maintained at all times to control mosquito breeding throughout Louisiana, for even though the "Yellow Fever" carrying mosquito has all but been eradicated in this hemisphere, his pesky "Cousin and Cousine" have not; and their bite, though not lethal, can still be quite irritating.

Créoles of New Orleans

Cemeteries

Cities of the Dead! — coffins rising above the earth, stacked in tiers — the design has a most practical purpose; however; coffins placed directly into the ground could wash to the surface after heavy rains since the earth is nothing but swamp land.

The week prior to All Saints Day (the day following Halloween) is spent sprucing up the family plots, cutting the grass, pulling weeds, and white-washing the tombs. On All Saints Day, family members and old friends come to the graveyard to bring flowers and say prayers for the departed souls.

Until quite recently, coffee and gumbo (as well as flowers) were sold in the cemeteries on All Saints Day.

Many New Orleanians call Mardi Gras "Carnival Day" and the entire Carnival, "Mardi Gras." Many also say "Mardi Gras Day," but it is the Carnival Season, and the one day is "Mardi Gras." Mardi Gras! Fat Tuesday! Shrove Tuesday! — the day immediately preceding "Ash Wednesday" and the beginning of Lent.

On January 6, which is Twelfth Night, the first official Ball takes place. The Krewe of Twelfth Night Revelers hold their Ball then and mark the beginning of the Season, but during recent years increasingly more organizations have begun to hold Balls even before the Twelfth Night Revelers, thus breaking another old tradition.

Mardi Gras, the Feast before the Fast, is held in February some years and in March in others, thus sometimes giving celebrants sixty days in which to hold the dozens of Balls, or sometimes less than thirty days. The date is dependent upon which date Pope Gregory's calendar has established as the beginning of Lent in a given year.

The tradition is French. In 1699, Iberville, founder of New Orleans (along with Bienville), named a small bayou, located twelve miles from the mouth of the Mississippi River, "Bayou Mardi Gras," because he discovered the bayou on Shrove Tuesday.

By 1766, when Louisiana was under the Spanish rule of Governor Don Antonio De Ulloa, Mardi Gras was an established custom. The Spanish permitted it to continue for a few years, but then banned street masking on that day, even though the Carnival Balls continued, both private and public, to which one could purchase a ticket to attend and observe. They were discontinued in 1805, but then resumed again in 1823. Street masking was revived in 1835, and a Mardi Gras parade was first described in a newspaper in the city in 1838.

Many Balls and Parades are held in the final weeks that precede Mardi Gras, the day of masking and general "Revelry and Merriment." Balls and Parades are held almost nightly, and on the two weekends prior, Parades also "roll" in the daytime as well.

The Carnival Season culminates its annual "Putting Away of Flesh" (meat) with a final fling, a donning of masks and costumes, and the celebrants dance and parade throughout the city streets. The Krewes of Rex and Zulu and countless decorated private club trucks that follow the King of Carnival (Rex's contingent of floats) roll in the day; and the Krewe of Comus traditionally parades in the evening, signifying the end of the "merrymaking" for another year. Midnight, when the two Krewes meet (Rex and Comus), marks the beginning of Lent, Ash Wednesday.

The celebration is not a commercial enterprise in any way, though hotels and merchants do a thriving business because of it. The city government has nothing to do with the festivities nor does the Chamber of Commerce. Carnival organizations and private clubs with strictly limited memberships pay all the bills. However, the city does encourage and aid by building grandstands and protecting the vast numbers of tourists and community members that attend the parades and visit the city.

On Ash Wednesday, the Catholic faithful, in token of penitence, can be seen wearing on their foreheads smudges of ashes given them by their priests, sometimes while still wearing traces of yesterday's make-up on their faces and bits of confetti in their hair.

Parades

Parades in the Seventh Ward??!!
"The Jolly Bunch" . . . comes through from the sixth ward . . .
The "Zulu" Parade in May
"The New Orleans Créole Fiesta" . . . in May
Parades . . . ????!!
"The Indians" on Mardi Gras Day. . . .

Parades . . . !!!??

The whistle blows
The drummers roll
Trombones pump rhythm up and down
Hands start clappin'
Feet start stompin'
The parade is movin' movin' goin' uptown

Horns start honkin'
Motors racing
Taps on marching boots are scraping
Batons twirl and fly
The parade is movin' movin' movin'
Goin' goin' uptown

Wheels start turning
Arms are dancing
Drums are pushing
Throbbing beating
Movin' movin' movin'
Goin'
We're goin' uptown

See me goin' uptown
Watch me struttin' uptown
Dancin' drummin' tapping flowing
Goin' goin' goin' uptown
Smilin' goin' uptown
Wavin' goin' uptown
Laughin' shakin' struttin' dancin'
Movin' movin'
Goin' goin' uptown
Goin'
Goin' goin'
Goin' uptown.

The New Orleans Creole Fiesta Association

"May your reign be rich and popular and may your friends adore you!! Queen Charlotte Morgan . . . King Theodore Joseph Lessassier . . . May you rule happily over the Creole City for one year. Congratulations your Creole Majesties!!"
The New Orleans Créole Fiesta Association
Annual Ball . . . April 1978
(King's Party following the Parade)

"Les Cavaliers Attendent a la Fête"
(The New Orleans Creole Fiesta Association)

"Mesdemoiselles Dansent a la Fête"
(The New Orleans Creole Fiesta Association)

Madame a la Fête, Hilda Rose
(The New Orleans Creole Fiesta Association)

Créoles of New Orleans

Creole Babies with Flashin' Eyes

"A Créole is any person of European descent born in the West Indies or Spanish America; a person descended from or culturally related to the original French settlers of the southern United States, especially Louisiana; the French patois spoken by these people; a person descended from or culturally related to the Spanish and Portuguese settlers of the Gulf States; a person of Negro descent born in the Western hemisphere, as distinguished from a Negro brought from Africa, also called "Créole Negro"; any person of mixed European and Negro ancestry who speaks a Créole dialect. (French Créole, from Spanish Crillo, from Portuguese. Negro born in his master's house, from Criar, to bring up, from Latin Creare, to create, to beget.)"

This definition of Créole is from the *American Heritage Dictionary of the English Language.*

Anthony Stanton
"I don't meet any ugly people! I think your ways make you beautiful . . . your personality . . . I never meet any strangers!"

*Joyce Morgan and her daughters at the
New Orleans Creole Fiesta King's Party 1978*

The Lesassier sisters at the
New Orelans Creole Fiesta King's Party 1978

Créoles of New Orleans

Barroom Visionaries in Joe Hobbs' Bar

You could feed all the pure white people in New Orleans with a half a pound of beans and a half a cuppa rice!

"My mother's father fed Morrison's people in Pointe Coupee. They were next door neighbors. My mother's father used to be a blacksmith. Morrison's family didn't have food to eat, but by him being white he was able to go to LSU on scholarship with his father's help and all. And you know, as things changed after the depression came up and all, he became a politician.

Joe Hobbs

"My grandfather used to feed them. They didn't have food to eat. My grandmother made biscuits, and Grandfather always had crops in the fields, and he did his blacksmithin' on the side, and he used to sell ice cream and all outside of church on Sundays. So *he* had when nobody else had, and he'd swap horseshoes for a hamper of potatoes and like that. . . .

"My ma would say, 'Allez coucher!' And that means 'Get out!' "

"Get out?"

"Yeah! 'Allez coucher! Get out!' "

"But, in French that means 'Go to bed!' "

"Oh yeah??! Always thought it meant 'Get out!' My ma would say it. Kinda broken language down here, huh?!

"In my family we finished college. My father finished. And all his brothers finished college. Now that goes way, way back! You go to Palestine, Texas, you'll find Alonzo Marion Story High School! He was the great uncle of a citizen of the seventh ward. Right now! He was just buried about eight years ago at the age of ninety-six. Finished from the University of Kansas in 1890 . . . somethin! He couldn't find a job here, so he went to Texas to find a job and became principal of this school. After he retired as principal he taught the blind, taught the Braille System, and they named that huge school after him . . . and that was before integration. On a big hill right there in Palestine, Texas. He was related to 'Alderman' Story, you know? The politician 'Story' who was responsible for Storyville, for making the red light district all together over on Basin Street and all! Same family from the seventh ward. Storyville was named for him."

"My grandfather finished from Leeland College, and all his sisters and brothers finished from college."

"The Créole families sent their children to Xavier Prep — uptown. St. Aug is new . . . just since the early 50's."

"And the Holy Family!! You forgot that!"

"Yeah! The Holy Family. That was where the Bourbon Orleans Hotel is now, and where they used to have those Octaroon Balls. That was a grand ballroom for prostitutes, ya hear!!? Octaroons . . . an eighth! Well, that's called Free Jacks. In other words they had the right to go wherever they wanted to. Free men of color! The Octaroon Ballroom was owned by Free Jacks! You see!? The one they gave the Sisters of the Blessed Sacrament. The Sisters taught us Créoles."

"That's why I say City Hall's got all of this downstairs in the basement. They don't want to think about it though. Yeah! Everybody in New Orleans all mixed up . . . lotta mixed up blood lines!"

"Sisters of the Blessed Sacrament, nuns — white nuns from France — taught us all at Corpus Christi School. A nun out of Cornwall, Pennsylvania dedicate her life to teaching . . . well, in those days they said "colored." She was a 'Swift' — more money than you could shake a stick at — Mother Catherine Drexel. That lady was my idol. She donated the ground to Xavier for the school. I knew her when I was at Xavier University. I knew her when I was at Xavier Prep, too. A saint, that woman. We learned the Golden Rule from those wonderful nuns. 'Do unto others as you would have others do unto you!"

"Huey Long said, 'You can feed all the pure white persons in New Orleans with a loaf of bread and a pound of red beans and still have food left over.' He said that cause he was afraid of this big time New Orleans gangster who he had called a nigger and then corrected his statement that 'the gangster was a nigger. . . .' Course this gangster was born as colored but later on went as white. Oh Huey Long loved to get skeletons in your closet. He was a manipulator."

Chuck: "I remember when Huey Long died. I was five years old. I mean, I saw tears on everybody's face! That's how much they loved that man. Nobody likes to see a good person die, especially if you are in an oppressed world. He was good to the people."

Barroom Visionaries — Jimmy Dorsey

T he window fan drones. The street noises are far away.
The barroom is empty and spacious. It has tile floors and a
twenty-two foot long tiled bar front. Rows of pint bottles of liquor
five bottles deep and twenty bottles long line the back bar. Seven
shelves of evenly spaced pint bottles of bourbon, scotch, rye, gin, and vodka
stand waiting. The door and the windows are wide open to catch the breeze.
Black iron bars cover each opening.

Jimmy Dorsey

The bar owner, Jimmy Dorsey, is a seventy-five year old 'ladies man.' He
attends customers in his filtered day lit and shadowy bar. The enormous window fan pulls the hot breeze in from the outside and cools it as it streams over
the slick cold tiles.

Chuck, Owen and I watch Dorsey, who carefully pours liquor into shot
glasses and prepares a drink for each of us. Dorsey leans against his back bar
of glass liquor filled soldiers, puffs on a fat cigar, turns a diamond ring around
his finger to face us, and begins to reminisce.

"Part of this back here in the Seventh Ward used to be swamp one time. That's the way it goes."

Chuck: "All that over there used to be a patio with tables and umbrellas."

"Don't have it any more. None of those outside places, watermelon stands and all . . . gone! Guess people got too cosmopolitan!

"I bought this place in 1940, 38 years ago! When I bought this, it was a dairy, cows and all."

Chuck: ". . . and St. Augustine was a farm, a one-man farm."

"I'm seventy-five years old, born in 1903. I been workin' hard all my life. That's why I don't look my age."

(Everybody in the bar laughs.)

Chuck: "He's been a ladies' man all his life . . . all his life."

"Well, I'll tell you, it's just as cheap to be the ladies' man as to be a man's man! My definition of 'A Ladies' Man'?! Well, you meet a girl in the streets, and she's got nobody to look after her. You put her down and show her right from wrong. You school her! And you let her pay for it! That's the way the game goes. White boys do the same thing with um . . . take the girls out of school and show um right from wrong. They don't know wrong? And if they don't want to listen? You pay for your learnins'. Then you be a smart girl! All you got to do is have understandins'. . . . Think that's the right game?"

(I don't know?! It sounds right for you. How long have you been a Ladies' Man?)

"Well, it's been my life all the way through — this and rooming houses. This the best game for me. Gamble, roomin' houses — that the best life! See! That way they don't be no 'I say' and 'You say'. You always got a place to feed the girls, and they got somethin' to get at all time. . . . see? So I don't have no troubles. That's the onliest way you can make some money — gamblin' and girls! Course gamblin' — you got to put out . . . calls for a bankroll at all times. I been in this game since I was about thirteen years old."

Chuck: "Tell um about Rampart Street, Jim! Tell um about the High Yellas!"

"Rampart Street was rough, Miss! It was rough. Canal Street was rough! See, they had bad girls and good girls out on Rampart Street. It was the Bucks. White and black was on the street. That was Tom Anderson. . . . And that's the way that game works."

"And Basin Street was the same way. Basin Street all them white girls and colored girls — one on this street and one on that street — they standin'

in doors all night. Next mornin' they'd show up with some money, and if they'd go to jail, they man would get um out. So! That's the way this life was built up, and it never will stop. Never!!

"Rampart Street was no angel! They didn't have no band of music like there is now. Used to be an old broken piano, and you'd play the piano. Fun all night long, and they'd never worry about it. This life never owed um' nothin'! Some of um get kilt. Some of um get beat up . . . to death. . . .

"The seventh ward wasn't bad then. It's worser now since the Project come in. This was a quiet neighborhood. Always a quiet ward. Never had much trouble down here. Sixth and fifth wards was bad!

"I come down here around 1925, but I never stayed down here then. I was from Dumaine and Claiborne. That's sixth ward."

Chuck: "Tell her about what color of skin used to live down this way. Tell her about the Créoles."

"Well! All the Créole peoples was nice and "bright" down here, and you had to have some get up and go about yourself. If you wasn't a good dresser, a nice man, knowed some trade or somethin', you'd never. . . . Well, you'd never get cut in. And the girls — they ain't no angels. There ain't no one woman that's more than the other woman.

"People down here tell you right straight! They don't have no headache here! This place never was no black and tan! It was always "bright" people here in the seventh ward!

"I'm born and raised in New Orleans. New Orleans never gave me nothin'."

Dorsey went to unlock the iron barred gate that stood locked against most would-be customers. Chuck tells us that Jim Dorsey was the "odd fellow" when he moved into the Créole section and bought property. He was darker complexioned than the Créoles; however, he reassures us that there was "no trouble" at that time over Dorsey's moving into their neighborhood.

Chuck: "You want to see back there?" He pointed toward the back of the building. He and I went into the non-functioning kitchen, situated in an added-on shed. Beyond that were two dice tables, carefully covered with sheets of heavy clear plastic.

We entered a door to the left of "The Dice Room," and I found myself in what seemed to be an apartment, but turned out to be three carefully furnished bedrooms or "Cribs" as Dorsey called them. Each "Crib" had a queen-sized bed, a dresser and a chair, and one window covered with a plastic shower curtain. One curtain was a ruby-red color. The sunshine filtering through it gave the room a red glow. The second room was bathed in a filtered blue plastic light. The third was shimmering in amber plastic — all very sleazy and cool, very effectively other worldly on a swelteringly hot June afternoon in New Orleans.

The girls who belonged to the "Cribs" were nowhere to be seen, neither in the apartment nor in the bar. There was no action at the dice tables. The sun was burning white and hot outside.

"New Orleans was no angel! Everything went on in New Orleans!"

(What about today?)

"Same way! The white and the black been goin' on! White people, white boys, white girls, black people, black boys, black girls . . . all of um mixed together in New Orleans! Right here! You'd be surprised to know how many of these white mens took care of these colored girls here. And that life *never* will stop! Yeah! Plenty white boys didn't have nowhere to flop . . . like Roccaforte! He didn't have nowhere to stay, and I led him out. A colored lady took him. 'Say! Come on. I'll bring you on Roman Street between Conti and Bienville.' He give her a place. He treated her nice. Before he died he always look out for her. Give her this and give her that. But in 1923, he didn't have nothin'!"

Dorsey relights his cigar and puffs on it.

"Oh! Yeah! This town has changed plenty! You don't know who's who today! Everything goes on. People leavin' and comin' down this way. You got so many you don't know who they is!

"Years ago people used to stay in their own neighborhoods and territories. But, no more! Now they all go everywhere. Everywhere you go you see different. You see white, black, Chinamen, Jewmen, every damn thing!

"This town here? Well! I'll tell ya we always had good lookin' women down here in this neighborhood, back a town! Sound like I'm a radio when I go to talkin', huh?!

"Well, I'll tell you. What didn't worry my life isn't worthwhile havin'. Ain't no money fallin' off the trees! You got to get out there and use your head for more than a hat rack!

"Oh! You had some dark skin back in here. Well they stood in their bunch. A while, lot of um had kinfolks here. You see the collector jumped over the fence. You understand? One favor deserve another one. If it idn't worth- while askin' it idn't worthwhile havin'.

"I used to be in the French Market all night — gamble, buy stuff, sell stuff. Sell it make money. That's the way I came up. I never had no trouble like. . . . Say! I got to go to Bourbon Street when integration passed up. I done forget all them burglers out there. I'm comin' back of town!

"Yeah! I know on . . . Villere Street . . . Viola! Viola was a cute little trick. Little brown-skin girl. Viola came down nice lookin' . . . coal black hair. White Johnny crazy about her. Kept her in the Deauville! Johnny — good hustler — cards, poker, dice, gettin' in Jefferson Parish and make money there. You know, he an all around guy. Kept that bankroll and had good men to do favors for. And anyway some money involved like with this guy in the French Market. Anywhere they needed some money they get it . . . you know? Shucks! He went and let her go! When Johnny died, she the one put him in the grave. He was a white boy, but he was crazy about Vi. And every- body — all the boys in the Red Light District — we all knowed what was goin' on. We didn't care. They had people . . . different people griping, but she wanted to be with him. That's her. But, he never let her do no time. He kept her and he never worked. Didn't do nothin' but gamble.

"Oh! You can make some money! Ain't no days go by, baby, when you catch a Norwegian ship, and you can put down some dead weight. When them ships come from Italy, foreign countries . . . deep water boats."

(Dorsey chuckles to himself.)

"Oh! I could tell you. . . . I say . . . (Dorsey can't continue because he is laughing so hard) . . . I seen these people go . . . Garpple . . . Gaaaa Gobble . . . I don't know what he be talkin' about. . . . But I got his money! Oh! Yeah!"

Storyville

Alderman Sydney Story sponsored the ordinance whereby a *"restricted district" or "red light district" was to be set aside in which prositution was to be considered "legal," and where all the prostitutes in the city were to be confined. The City Council passed the ordinance on January 26, 1897.*

The district came to be known as "Storyville," a dubious honor for Sydney Story. Therein "Jazz" is said to have been born, in the many parlors of the "Houses" and in the saloons, which also offered nightly musical entertainment to their patrons.

Storyville was closed in 1917. The buildings were demolished in the late 1930's and early 40's, then a public housing project was erected.

The Old Circle Movie Theatre

"**T**he seventh ward is changing. It's changing right now. The young people don't want to be watched, scrutinized . . . eyes of the neighbors and all. . . Want to come and go, do as they please! So they move. No Aunties to tell Mama, no cousins to tell Uncle or Parain. Mais! Do as you please! They're movin' out to New Orleans East."

The future of the seventh ward? Don't quote me . . .
It will become more and more of the inner-city
Only the old will be left here
The old and the poor
The young are moving
Moving out
(To East New Orleans?)
Yes! They used to call it a swamp
Yes! Out in East New Orleans

There's Caesar's East . . . and Cisco's out there. . . .

The wonderful Boys Club?
That's down the street here
But! There is a new club
It's called the Spartan's Social and Pleasure Club
New members from all around the city
Not just the seventh ward
You tend to hang out with guys you went to school with
And they live all over now not just in the seventh ward now
The city's gotten a lot bigger now
More open easier
Not just black places and white places
Anybody can go any place they want now
Any place
Lots of space

Clarence Carr
"New Orleans has improved so much. That's why I'm moving back here from New York. I plan to open a restaurant. It's the most fascinating city in the world and I've been around the world 32 times. Now, I don't say this just because I was born here. . . . There's nothing like the hospitality of the beautiful people in this city. Unique! People are divided everywhere but not here . . . not here!"

Yes! I grew up in the seventh ward
Yes! My wife grew up in the seventh ward
Yes! My daughter was born in the seventh ward
But! We moved out to the spaces
We needed more spaciousness . . .
A newer type construction we couldn't find in the seventh ward
Yes! I'm French background and black
So is my wife
Créole?
(He laughs) No! I'm not a Créole
What is a Créole?
I like to look in the dictionary for definitions
But! . . . French and black descent. . . .
A person of French and black descent
(Aren't you a Créole then?!)
No! I'm *not* a Créole
By definition it connotes people who did not want to be black

(Do you belong to the Bon Ton Club? The New Orleans Créole
Fiesta Assn?)
Noooo! I don't belong to social and pleasure clubs
(Not the Bon Ton not the Autocrat Club?)
Yes! Did I say I didn't belong to the Autocrat. . . .
I do go there on occasion. . . . Yes! I do belong to the Autocrat
Club

(Do you go to the jazz spots . . . the discos?)
No! Wellll . . . my position . . . it wouldn't speak well of me

Charles Story

What is a Créole? The following are definitions from Webster, the American Heritage, Dimsa's Spanish-English, and the Larousse French-English Dictionaries:

History Sketch Book and Guide to New Orleans and Environs published New York, Will H. Coleman, No. 70, Business Quarter, Astor House 1885.

"To them (San Dominguais) is due the word "créole" to express the native Louisianian of French and Spanish descent. The word was originally Spanish and applied only to the American descendants of Spaniards; but it spread to the French West Indies and was brought by the San Domingians to Louisiana."

French *Créole* from Spanish *Criollo*; from Portuguese *Crioulo*. Negro born in his master's house. From *criar*, to bring up; from Latin *creare*, to create, beget, to produce.

Any person of European descent born in the West Indies or Spanish America.

A person descended from or culturally related to the original French settlers of the southern United States, especially Louisiana. The French patois spoken by these people.

A person descended from or culturally related to the Spanish and Portuguese settlers of the Gulf States.

A person of Negro descent born in the western hemisphere as distinguished from a Negro brought from Africa . . . also called a Créole Negro.

Any person of mixed European and Negro ancestry who speaks a Créole dialect.

A white person descended from the French or Spanish settlers of Louisiana and the Gulf States and preserving their characteristic speech and culture.

A person of mixed Créole and Negro blood speaking a dialect of French and Spanish. A half-breed.

Criollio: A Spaniard born in the Americas. Adj. indigenous.

Lunch at Eddie's Restaurant with "Chuck"

"The seventh ward is noted for the tradesmen, bricklayers, roofers, carpenters, you know, mostly technical people. They noted for they barbers, too.

"You wanna get the tempo of the seventh ward? This is probably what you'd call your 'hard hat ward.'"

(Was it always that way though?)

"Always!"

(What's your definition of Créole?)

"A Créole is a mixture of black and white. Now, that's what we call it. I know the real definition is Spanish and French. We don't call it like that."

(What do you consider the seventh ward to be?)

"O.K. It extends from St. Claude St. to the St. Bernard Project. . . . Yeah! From Esplanade to Elysian Fields to . . . I'm almost sure, now . . . to Gentilly."

(Were things more "jumpin" back here in the seventh ward at one time?)

"Well . . . there were little pockets. There were vacant lots and space. In the '40's during World War II the majority of people from the seventh ward moved out to California — migrated to L.A. in search of jobs in factories."

A singer on the Juke Box sings, "Spendin' My Life in This Limbo . . ."

"This section reminds me of the west side of L.A. They have the same traditions as here — the names of some of the spots. You got a St. Bernard Food Market over there, got a hot sausage factory over there, Olivier's. . . ."

(There's a large New Orleans' Créole population in L.A.?)

"Everybody I grew up with . . . yeah! It's like my second home. I'm gettin' ready to go for a visit."

The pick-up order bell rings and continues to ring. Steaming platters of fried oysters with two ice cream scoop mounds of spicy potato salad pass by our table. Lettuce and pickles, fried filet of fresh trout platters glide by in a long procession, all held aloft by the waitresses. The juke box singer continues his song . . . "Spendin' My Life in This Limbo. . . ."

(Most of your contemporaries are out in L.A.?)

"Yes! Yes! Howard Coignet lived out there and came back. Out there eleven years and came back."

(Have many come back?)

The singer continues . . . "Tryin' So Hard to Reach My Goal. . . ."

"Some of them are tricklin' back. The south has opened up. Trouble is, plenty of them have families over there, families that have been reared in California. That California style of livin' is very very very different from here."

(Do you like it?)

"I'm an adaptable person. Whenever my friend Claude says, 'Come on, let's go!' I'm gone."

(Tell me about some of the private clubs in New Orleans.)

"Well, Mr. Richard Gumble is one of the founders of the Autocrat Club. He's about 91 years old. He's probably over there right now. Every day you catch him at Miro and St. Bernard. Every day he catches that 3:15 bus. His grandson, you've seen him on ABC's Wide World of Sports . . . every week . . . little . . . uh . . . can't remember his first name. He's a commentator!

"Yeah! The Autocrat Club is about the biggest down here. I was in a political fight there and got out. I was young at the time. I'm sorry I got out. I was Secretary of the Club. And, 'Wonderful Boys' Club' wanted me to be President over there. I was also on the Urban League at the time . . . NAACP . . . I was into too much. I think that's what caused my divorce."

(What's the difference between the Autocrat and the Wonderful Boys Clubs?)

"A huge difference. The Autocrat Club was the epitome of the seventh ward! That's where all your Créole families and their sons and their sons belonged! It was a very clandestined Society 'til 1962 . . . as to the people they selected to join the organization. Until a young group got in (that was me!). And we opened it up! Wide! And the old men are still mad with me."

(What were the criteria for getting in the Club? Was it color?)

"You had to be bright! It was partly that . . . partly. And a name in the community. . . . I knew you and Owen were going to have a 'ball' at the Coignet Wedding Renewal Party. Great! Wonderful family. Generous and charming . . . filled with largesse!"

(Wonderful and generous.)

"This is typical of the seventh ward people. Generosity! In L.A. it's the same way . . . and their kids are growing up the same way . . . 'cause we love to give parties. We used to give suppers a long time ago. We shared, and you get a pleasure out of sharing! It must be from the French . . . or Catholics. . . . You know Corpus Christi Church is the second to largest Parish in the United States? The Credit Union there is the apple of my eye!

"The Credit Union *had* to be independent! Run like a business. Anyone who'd come up there to the Priest and give him a sob story, he'd just give them the money. Right now that Credit Union is worth 9 or 10 million."

(Sitting at another table two black women are talking. . . . "They're very cautious about blacks." The second one asks, "What do my ancestors represent?")

"You want to know the most important institutions in this ward?"

The Autocrat Club. But, the Vaucresson Meat Market right over there on St. Bernard Ave. Sonny had a booth over at the Jazz Fest. . . . Also, the Union Halls, the Carpenters Union Hall, Bricklayers Union Hall, Plasterers. Yeah! Plasterers . . . Carpenters and Bricklayers . . . When we finish lunch I'll show you where the Elite used to live."

(Who?)

"The Elite! The section they used to call Sugar Hill — right before you get to Dillard, right near where you used to live."

(On Pauger? Between Pleasure and Humanity Streets?")

"Right in that area."

(Do you think the Morial family considers itself Créoles?')

"Well! Look at him. What do you think?"

(Yes! I do. Does Dutch belong to the Autocrat Club?)

"I don't know, now. He belonged at one time."

Haspel's Clothing Store on St. Bernard Avenue

(Are the young people moving out of the seventh ward?)

"Yeah! They're going to the East . . . New Orleans East. There's a big population shift! When I was comin' up, my mother lived in the seventh ward, her father and mother lived in the seventh ward. Like that!"

(It's not like that any more?)

"No! That old tradition . . . in the same block your aunt lived and the grandmother lived, and the kids got married and found a house in the same block. Very little of it is left today. Kids want to move away from the family."

A black male blues singer is singing on the juke box . . . "To keep hangin' on / After the thrill has gone / Oh! Baby / To keep hangin' on after the thrill is gone . . ." The juke box winds down, we leave Eddie's,.and Chuck takes us on a nostalgia trip of his very own. He points out houses where he used to go to parties and houses where old girl friends lived and houses where old friends no longer live. We went on a sad pilgrimage.

The Autocrat Club
(A club exclusively for men. Started in 1914 and chartered in 1920.)

Créoles of New Orleans

Robert Meteyes

"My grandmother and her husband were from Brest, France. My grandfather's name was Meteyes. Yeah! They all mixed up.

"I joined the Autocrat Club in 1920. And if I still belonged, I'd be one of the oldest members.

"The Autocrat Club was started in 1914, chartered in 1920 or 21. You know why I got out? They didn't have a gymnasium.

"This is a men's club. All men! The St. Jacento Club, too — beautiful club — was on 1422 Dumaine St. Eleven hundred members. Had my own locker. We all had our own lockers. Beautiful arena. Had boxing every Sunday. Used to box there.

"I'm a retired 'rounder' at night. Used to be I could leave any barroom 3 or 4 o'clock in the mornin'! Walk home just like I was walkin' in my own house. Don't have nothin' on your mind. But, today you can't step out that door somebody don't grab you. I mean *that* could happen anywhere! So, I stay home now. So, they grab me in the daytime. You can do the same thing in the day you can do at night! That's all right. . . . More of it!

"You could pass in the alleys, pass anywhere! Nobody out . . . safe!"

(You have an accent!?)

"Well, that's all they used to speak to me. Speak French. My mother . . . I used to speak that way with them . . . until she died."

(What kind of work do you do?)

"Nothin! I please myself."

(You're retired?)

"I traveled for 46 years and 6 months for a pullman company."

(What pullman company?)

"Every train that they had out of here."

(Where did you travel?)

"All over the United States."

(Did you like it?)

"I loved it! Made me what I am today. Now, I'm ridin' planes! Plane took me two nights ago to L.A. Now, I go over there in four hours. Eat breakfast here in the morning and supper over there, come home the same evening.

"I retired in sixty-nine. I'm seventy-nine years old. My baby's sixty! My *baby*! Nine grandchildren, fourteen great-grandchildren. All my family don't live here now.

"I go by L.A. and see my daughter, and a son in Chicago, Claude, and a niece in El Dorado, Texas.

"I was born and mostly raised in the seventh ward. Now I'm in the ninth ward, though."

(Why did you move?)

"Oh! Guess God willed it. As things change you know . . . My daughter went over there; my mother died and so forth; my wife's from over there, and she went back."

(You like it better?)

Robert Meteyes

Créoles of New Orleans

"I tell you what it is. I was married twenty-nine years, and we divorced twenty-three years. She remarried, and I remarried. Her husband died; my wife died.

"My first wife and I, we remarried in 1974. We would be married, right now, fifty-six years. We had three children. We divorced.

"When we married, my wife was sixteen years old, and I, twenty-one. Alfred Coignet Sr. was our best man in 1920. My wife and daughter were at the Coignet's wedding vow renewal party with me.

"The twenty-three years in between? . . . Well, we just tried to forget them all. My wife was livin' with my daughter, and I started to go and see her, see? My wife's name is Judith."

(What a wonderful story.)

"Oh, the priest thought it was the most wonderful, beautiful thing he ever heard. Twenty-three years divorced and remarried."

(Married for four years now?)

"Newlyweds! She's seventy-four, and I'm seventy-nine. And we both young in the yard! Have a garden. Yeah!"

(What's the secret of staying young?)

"Exercise! Umm hmm!"

(What kind?)

"Walkin'! Jumpin' rope! Lotta exercise."

(You smoke.)

"I smoked ever since I was big enough to pick up a butt."

(You drink, too?)

"Yeah! A little. . . . I inhaled cigarettes 'til I was thirty years old, and I took these (cigars)!

"Had the worst storm we ever had in history in 1915 — right here in New Orleans . . . a hurricane. A lot of homes blew down over here. Majority of all the homes was damaged. We got a break; never had no damage. Never did hear about the storm of 1915? Hmmm!"

"I came back from Los Angeles in 1957. I promised the Lord if He ever let me get out of Los Angeles, I'd never go back again. And I have never been back since."

"Place I don't care about is Chicago! Know my place? New York City!"

"New York's all right for a visit, also. . . . I ain't never found any place beat New Orleans!"

"Neither have I."

"You right."

"No! No!"

"I been all over the United States, and this the best place *I* ever been in!"

(What's your definition of a Créole?)

"Like us! I'm supposed to be a Créole! Umm! Partly French! And good Créole cook! Créole cookin'!"

Note: Robert Meteyes was interviewed at the bar of the Autocrat Club.

A Conversation with the Rouzans

A conversation with Mr. and Mrs. Harold Sidney Rouzan (Helen Le Blanc Rouzan), one of their daughters, well-known New Orleans singer Wanda Rouzan (Brazile), and her teen-aged daughter, Sydney Marie Brazile.

Mr. and Mrs. Sidney Rouzan; one of their daughters, the well-known New Orleans singer and performer Wanda Rouzan (Brazile); and her daughter, Sydney Marie Brazile.

The name Rouzan, is that a French name?

Mr. Rouzan: French and Spanish.

(Will you give me your definition of the word "Créole"?)

Mr. Rouzan: My definition of Créole? It's a mixture of French and Spanish people.

Mrs. Rouzan: I'll go a little further than him. My definition of Créole is a mixture of black, Indian, French, and Spanish. Maybe I should have said African. I don't know. As a child, I always remembered them using the word Créole, and those were the four colors. Now, you very seldom hear of the black connected. Now! You want the truth?

(Yes!)

Mrs. Rouzan: So, I'll have to give it to you. I mean, Créoles were there whether they were wanted or not. I think . . . It was a long time ago, I was a little girl, I think it was in our dictionary, those four colors. I noticed since my children grew up and went to school and everything, I don't see the "black" in there. As a youngster it was there. I think it's a mixture of races.

(Do you all speak French?)

Mr. Rouzan: No.

Wanda Rouzan and a Portrait of her Great-Grandmother

(When you were growing up? As children?)

Mr. Rouzan: My grandmother, my mother, yes! They spoke it. My older brother spoke it, and my grandmother on my mother's side could not speak English very well. She spoke French and Créole. That's two different languages. My mother spoke French and Créole. I only know a few words and phrases. Comment sa va? Sa va bien. Et vous?

Mrs. Rouzan: New Orleans is really a mixed-up city.

(Are you all from New Orleans?)

Mrs. Rouzan: Yes! I'm born here. He is also. Our parents were born here, too.

Mr. Rouzan: I'm born and raised in the seventh ward.

Mrs. Rouzan: I, too.

(How do you think the Créole culture has affected you in your life?)

Mrs. Rouzan: I don't feel that it's done anything to me. I've done everything that I've wanted to do. Maybe my husband felt more pressure of being segregated, because he was more out, on business and here and there.

Mr. Rouzan: Yes! In those days the word "black" was a fighting word. As "Negroes" we were affected, sometimes even now because of our color. The "blacks" don't always get along with us too well. They criticise us, that "we want to be white." That sort of stuff.

(Did you then find prejudice from both sides?)

Mr. Rouzan: Oh, yes!

Mrs. Rouzan: We're caught in the middle.

Mr. Rouzan: That's exactly right.

Mrs. Rouzan: We are!

Mr. Rouzan: In Plaquemines Parish, a section near Port Sulphur, they had a black church, a church for Créoles and one for whites. Same with the schools, up until the 60's. The whites didn't want the Créoles, and the Créoles didn't want the blacks; so they had to have three churches . . . Diamond, Louisiana.

(Sounds just like some of the theatres in New Orleans in the 1800's.)

Mrs. Rouzan: I feel there's a lot of that still exists around Louisiana. It isn't spoken of much. A lot of people feel they've been hurt or hindered in their strive to make their lives better. I didn't see it.

(Directed to Sydney, Wanda's thirteen year old daughter: You're the younger generation. How has being a Créole affected you?)

Sydney: Oh, I don't know. Now I'm able to relate to white people, because before I was never surrounded by them. I was surrounded by Créoles and blacks. I'm able to get along with everyone. I don't have any bad feelings. I feel that we're all one.

(Do you think of yourself as being a Créole?)

Sydney: I do. But, if someone asked me what color I was, I would say I was black, not Créole. But what I think? I think I am Créole. But, I'm also black. It's just really weird. It's just a mixture of a lot of things.

Mrs. Rouzan (breaks in laughing): It's weird! Huh, darling?

Wanda: When I started researching black language patterns, which is what my master's thesis was on, I did research on Créole patois and how our language evolved from West Africa; we grew up as Negroes, and at that time we had our own culture. We didn't veer too very far from that culture.

(You don't think your culture is very different from the black culture?)

Créoles of New Orleans

Wanda: Yes! We stayed within this group for the most part. When I got older and branched uptown to school at Xavier Prep, I could see the differences. I became friendly with people from other wards, and there could be problems. You just didn't have that mingling then much, with the darker skinned blacks and the lighter skinned blacks. I have traveled — my child has, and so have my parents — all over the world. We don't consider that we live in a closed environment any more.

(Did you live in a closed environment?)

Wanda: Because of economics, too. We didn't have money to do a lot of things. We mainly entertained ourselves. We're a big family. We used to sing, my two sisters and I. My daddy and my mama's brother and my grandmother, we had our own entertainment right in our back yard here on this corner. The family would get together. We never needed anybody else. Our family would get together and go to the country.

(Do you think "the family" is one of the most important things in the Créole culture, society?)

Wanda: Absolutely!

Mrs. Rouzan: Oh, yes! That's the way it will always be!

Mr. Rouzan: It still is! There are so many ways the difference of being a Créole affected us. So many ways. Adversely sometimes, and sometimes it wasn't. Like our club, the Autocrat Club. I've been a member since 1936. You had black Créoles here in the seventh ward. My mother's sister was darker than her, but she spoke Créole. From her accent you could tell she was Créole. My grandmother on my mother's side was dark skinned, but she could barely speak English. She was more like my wife, Indian and French. My father's side, my father was as white as you. My grandfather looked like an Irishman, blue eyes. Now back to the Autocrat Club. You hardly ever found a black skinned person in the club. They didn't take them in. The only way a black Créole got in was if he knew somebody and he had beautiful hair. Nice hair if he was black. Maybe had two or three in a club of over 300 members. Now! They had bronze skinned Créoles, and white skinned Créoles. Lot of fellows in the club were so white they took advantage and crossed over. They did it for the purpose of their income.

Mrs. Rouzan: Their livelihood and to live. Look at when they rode the bus. Their black cousin would be sitting in the back of it, and the one that crossed over would be sitting in front, and they'd be just a wavin'. That's the way it was here.

(Is the Autocrat Club the same today?)

Mr. Rouzan: Changed completely.

Mrs. Rouzan: Oh, my God! That's so dead!

Mr. Rouzan: It changed in the 60's. Now, you have more blacks than white looking Créoles. Yes! Changed completely. Used to have certain carnival clubs where black skinned people could not get in.

Mrs. Rouzan: All of that's gone with the wind. That was a long time ago.

Wanda: A long time ago when you said "Créole," I dare not say that, because the darker skinned blacks would frown upon that. We were just Negroes. As I got to college, I know what I am. I'm black, because I've been raised that way all my life. But I also know what *part* of my ancestry was, I mean I couldn't pin it down. We couldn't even go pass "great-grand's," you know? But, now I say I'm a black Créole, and I don't have a problem saying it, because I know where my heart is. I know where my culture is, and I respect that.

(At one time it was as dangerous to say to a black, "I am a Créole of Color" as it was to say that to a white?)

Wanda: Yes.

(Mrs. Rouzan, what was your maiden name?)

Mrs. Rouzan: Le Blanc.

(French. Any Spanish in your family?)

Mrs. Rouzan: No! But, I only know what they say. They say my grandfather was an Indian. Don't know which tribe. Great-Grandmother was a Jackson Free, a Free Jack.

(Was World War II a big turning point?)

Mrs. Rouzan: It was!

Mr. Rouzan: After it my whole family went to California. I'm the only member of my immediate family here. My mother, sisters and brothers all went. I decided to stay in New Orleans. I was doing pretty well in the insurance business.

(Do they consider themselves to be Créoles?)

Mr. Rouzan: My sisters moved in to a black culture. My older brother continued as a Créole, never says he's black; my youngest brother, who lives in Compton, is a clown. He might say he is Créole, he might say he is white. He's pretty fair complexioned. He just might say anything. He lives as black.

(Do you all feel that as Créoles you hold a special place in history, that you are special?)

Wanda: I feel special as a person.

Mr. Rouzan: I feel proud of it myself!

Wanda: I feel proud of it, because I have had the benefit of a beautiful mixture. People say, "Girl! Where do you get all that soul?!" Because I can get down. Where I came from I came second lining, didn't get the gospel because we were Catholics, but I got that later on because I met with people who had those roots.

(So you do appreciate your special place in history?)

Wanda: I'm glad that people are finally finding out and researching and are getting more of the truth. But, there are so many skeletons in the closets. . . . But, if we could really put it down. . . .

Mrs. Rouzan: New Roads, Louisiana? All up there. . . . One big happy family up in there.

(What do you feel to be the most distinctive and interesting part of your life as a Créole?)

Mrs. Rouzan: The heritage here says, that's your sister, and she is a maid in Mrs. so and so's house; and that's your brother, he's a Doctor at Touro. And the other one has part of a political career, and it is wonderful to know that even though different people come out of one family, they still recognize and love one another dearly. Now! That's what I enjoy about the city of New Orleans. And know that no one passes one another up. So you're a maid? Well, that's your business, but you are my sister. Now I'm way up there, but I can come off of that high horse. I can come down and meet you anywhere, anytime, any place, in front of anybody. That's what I love about my life. Now that's my life, and I sort of feel that others are exactly the same way. It's a wonderful heritage. I don't give a damn if it is all mixed up! That's the way it goes!

Créoles of New Orleans

Mr. Rouzan: It took me a long time to realize that I was different from other people. We had white neighbors, and we lived together. They ate at my table, and I ate at their table. We were children. As we grew up, my white friends went one way, you know, and they failed to recognize me any more. This affected me in some way. I'd meet them in different parts of the city, and they'd make as if they didn't know me, and we had the same thing that happened with some of our Créoles who crossed over to the white side. They'd see you and wouldn't recognize you. That sort of stuff . . . well, that affected me. One thing I like about being a Créole . . . I had some advantages, too. I had some privileges that I could enjoy same as the white people. There were times they mistook me for white, and I took advantage of it sometimes. Many times I was sort of tickled about that. I didn't do it for any job, but to go into places of amusement; I took advantage of it. Other than that I enjoyed my life as a Créole because of the fact I had two ways to look at it. One way, the white people frowning on me, and the other way with the black people frowning on me; and I was able to live through it and enjoy it.

Wanda: One of the biggest things for me growing up was when my father cooked. He is a wonderful cook. Our cooking was an important part of everything that we did. But, we grew up with "feasting" just like every other family in New Orleans. That was always a part.

Mr. Rouzan: That's another thing about being a Créole

Wanda: Mama came to Australia when I was singing with Vernel Bagneris (a relative) on a tour of "One Mo' Time," and she brought CDM coffee and grits, and they wouldn't let her through customs. They didn't know what grits were; and my filé! In my travels that's what I *have* to bring.

(What is the favorite thing that you cook, Mr. Rouzan?)

Mr. Rouzan: Gumbo! Filé Gumbo! That's my specialty. I like that. We cook a big pot whenever we cook.

Wanda: And don't worry! When we cook it, the whole family comes over! (Everyone laughs.) And friends too! Coon and rabbit! Daddy likes to hunt, too.

(Do you find that most Créole homes were structured in such a fashion that the women stayed home?)

Mrs. Rouzan: Yes! That's what they did. They don't do it now. Everybody works. And there was respect for old folks. Still is!

Wanda: There was always the tradition. First Communion! In families there was a big celebration with food. They made calas, the rice cakes, and always had special foods associated with special occasions.

Mrs. Rouzan: Cowan and gumbo!

Wanda: I'm nostalgic. . . .

Mrs. Rouzan: I have to fight her 'cause all of the pictures of our family up in the attic are not for her!

Wanda: I'm nostalgic. . . .

Maude Randolph
" 'Do unto other as you would have others do unto you.'them
"That's the golden rule my generation was taught . . . and so we shared.
"If you have a pot beans . . . share it and enjoy it!"

Créoles of New Orleans

What is a Créole?

A true Créole?! What the white didn't want and the black man couldn't have   . . . a Créole . . . a house girl.

French, Italian, and Negro . . . Heinz . . . 57 varieties.

Créoles? Do Créoles have to be black now? We're Créoles!

The seventh ward seems to be a lot of things it is not . . . never was . . . and some things that it will never be again. . . . It is a neighborhood with a past and a present that has remained mysterious, perhaps intentionally. . . . To protect itself from outsiders . . . the whites, and the blacks as well. . . . For both never really seemed to fit in the Créole society . . . and indeed the Créole of Color never really seemed to fit in the white or the black society either. . . . And like so many groups of foreigners in a foreign land, the Créole bound itself together with its own traditions

family

language

food

and secrecy.

There are no longer many whites in New Orleans, nor in the world, who call themselves or who think of themselves as Créoles. There are however, people of mixed ancestry in Louisiana, in New Orleans, people of black, white and Indian heritage who still call themselves . . . Créoles.

Probably only in the city of New Orleans and in the "villes" of the West Indies in the 1700's and 1800's did such a full blown Créole society ever exist, a society that encompassed schools, churches, businesses, banks, insurance companies, stores and shops of all sorts, "pleasure clubs," debutante and carnival organizations, etc.; a hierarchy peopled with leaders, who along with their abilities to lead also had to possess the physical traits, characteristics, the finer qualities of both the white and the black races, and in the order of importance deemed necessary.

The Créole Society was graded by colors, shadings, tones, hues of colors, colors not purely white, not purely black; neither was desirable, but gradations, subtleties of aesthetics were what mattered — gentility, being refined, amiable, of good family, noble, and graceful.

Such a society flourished in New Orleans and still today exists, though not in so concentrated a form nor contained in what was once so condensed an area as the seventh ward.

A Créole Society does still exist in New Orleans. And if you are ever so fortunate as to be invited to attend one of their family gatherings or community events, go with the good grace to realize that you are one of the privileged few, who in these modern times has been able to partake of a life style born in more gentle days, a way of life perpetuated by the gracious spirit of the créoles aided by the bounty bestowed by nature upon all of the inhabitants of New Orleans.

Créoles of New Orleans

Hansen, Harry, editor, *A Guide to the State,* compiled by the Fed. Writer Program, WPA, State of La., Hastings House, N.Y. 1941.

Cogley, John, *Catholic America.*

Saxon, Lyle, *Fabulous New Orleans.*

Tallant, Robert, *Voodoo in New Orleans*

Cable, George W., *Dance in Place Congo,* Créole Slave Songs.

New Orleans City Guide, *Federal Writers Project,* Riverside Press, 1938.

Allain, Mme. Helene D'Aquin, *Souvenirs d'Amerique et de France par une Créole,* Nouvelle Maison a Paris.

Martineau, Harriet, *Society in America.*

Tallant, Robert, *Mardi Gras.*

Gayarré, Charles, History of Louisiana (American Domination) 1866 Edward O. Jenkins, Printer, New York

Special Acknowledgments:

J. B. Harter; Curator of Paintings and Prints, Louisiana State Museum

Robert R. Macdonald; former Director, Louisiana State Museum, currently Director of The Museum of The History of the City of New York.

G. Michael Strock: Park Historian; Jean Lafitte National Historical Park, Natl. Park Service, United States Dept. of Interior.

Oscar Lee Bates; Curator of Exhibitions, Louisiana State Museum.

Thomas B. Lemann

George deVille

Cover hand tinted by Tracy Smith

We are not implying that all of the people in the photographs contained in this book are Créoles, Créoles of Color, people of color, or even necessarily Caucasian. Within the boundaries of the Seventh Ward, people of all races, religions and nationalities are to be found.

The Authors